Ancient Egypt: A Very Short Introduction

VERY SHORT INTRODUCTIONS are for anyone wanting a stimulating and accessible way in to a new subject. They are written by experts, and have been published in more than 25 languages worldwide.

The series began in 1995, and now represents a wide variety of topics in history, philosophy, religion, science, and the humanities. Over the next few years it will grow to a library of around 200 volumes – a Very Short Introduction to everything from ancient Egypt and Indian philosophy to conceptual art and cosmology.

Very Short Introductions available now:

ANCIENT EGYPT   Ian Shaw
ANCIENT PHILOSOPHY
   Julia Annas
THE ANGLO-SAXON AGE
   John Blair
ANIMAL RIGHTS   David DeGrazia
ARCHAEOLOGY   Paul Bahn
ARCHITECTURE
   Andrew Ballantyne
ARISTOTLE   Jonathan Barnes
ART HISTORY   Dana Arnold
ART THEORY   Cynthia Freeland
THE HISTORY OF
   ASTRONOMY   Michael Hoskin
ATHEISM   Julian Baggini
AUGUSTINE   Henry Chadwick
BARTHES   Jonathan Culler
THE BIBLE   John Riches
BRITISH POLITICS
   Anthony Wright
BUDDHA   Michael Carrithers
BUDDHISM   Damien Keown
CAPITALISM   James Fulcher
THE CELTS   Barry Cunliffe
CHOICE THEORY
   Michael Allingham
CHRISTIAN ART   Beth Williamson
CLASSICS   Mary Beard and
   John Henderson
CLAUSEWITZ   Michael Howard
THE COLD WAR   Robert McMahon

CONTINENTAL PHILOSOPHY
   Simon Critchley
COSMOLOGY   Peter Coles
CRYPTOGRAPHY
   Fred Piper and Sean Murphy
DADA AND SURREALISM
   David Hopkins
DARWIN   Jonathan Howard
DEMOCRACY   Bernard Crick
DESCARTES   Tom Sorell
DRUGS   Leslie Iversen
THE EARTH   Martin Redfern
EGYPTIAN MYTH   Geraldine Pinch
EIGHTEENTH-CENTURY
   BRITAIN   Paul Langford
THE ELEMENTS   Philip Ball
EMOTION   Dylan Evans
EMPIRE   Stephen Howe
ENGELS   Terrell Carver
ETHICS   Simon Blackburn
THE EUROPEAN UNION
   John Pinder
EVOLUTION
   Brian and Deborah Charlesworth
FASCISM   Kevin Passmore
THE FRENCH REVOLUTION
   William Doyle
FREE WILL   Thomas Pink
FREUD   Anthony Storr
GALILEO   Stillman Drake
GANDHI   Bhikhu Parekh

GLOBALIZATION   Manfred Steger
HEGEL   Peter Singer
HEIDEGGER   Michael Inwood
HIEROGLYPHS   Penelope Wilson
HINDUISM   Kim Knott
HISTORY   John H. Arnold
HOBBES   Richard Tuck
HUME   A. J. Ayer
IDEOLOGY   Michael Freeden
INDIAN PHILOSOPHY
   Sue Hamilton
INTELLIGENCE   Ian J. Deary
ISLAM   Malise Ruthven
JUDAISM   Norman Solomon
JUNG   Anthony Stevens
KANT   Roger Scruton
KIERKEGAARD   Patrick Gardiner
THE KORAN   Michael Cook
LINGUISTICS   Peter Matthews
LITERARY THEORY
   Jonathan Culler
LOCKE   John Dunn
LOGIC   Graham Priest
MACHIAVELLI   Quentin Skinner
MARX   Peter Singer
MATHEMATICS   Timothy Gowers
MEDIEVAL BRITAIN
   John Gillingham and
   Ralph A. Griffiths
MODERN IRELAND   Senia Pašeta
MOLECULES   Philip Ball
MUSIC   Nicholas Cook
MYTH   Robert A. Segal
NIETZSCHE   Michael Tanner
NINETEENTH-CENTURY
   BRITAIN   Christopher Harvie and
   H. C. G. Matthew
NORTHERN IRELAND
   Marc Mulholland
PARTICLE PHYSICS   Frank Close
PAUL   E. P. Sanders
PHILOSOPHY   Edward Craig
PHILOSOPHY OF SCIENCE
   Samir Okasha

PLATO   Julia Annas
POLITICS   Kenneth Minogue
POLITICAL PHILOSOPHY
   David Miller
POSTCOLONIALISM
   Robert Young
POSTMODERNISM
   Christopher Butler
POSTSTRUCTURALISM
   Catherine Belsey
PREHISTORY   Chris Gosden
PRESOCRATIC PHILOSOPHY
   Catherine Osborne
PSYCHOLOGY   Gillian Butler and
   Freda McManus
QUANTUM THEORY
   John Polkinghorne
ROMAN BRITAIN
   Peter Salway
ROUSSEAU   Robert Wokler
RUSSELL   A. C. Grayling
RUSSIAN LITERATURE
   Catriona Kelly
THE RUSSIAN REVOLUTION
   S. A. Smith
SCHIZOPHRENIA
   Chris Frith and Eve Johnstone
SCHOPENHAUER
   Christopher Janaway
SHAKESPEARE   Germaine Greer
SOCIAL AND CULTURAL
   ANTHROPOLOGY
   John Monaghan and Peter Just
SOCIOLOGY   Steve Bruce
SOCRATES   C. C. W. Taylor
SPINOZA   Roger Scruton
STUART BRITAIN   John Morrill
TERRORISM   Charles Townshend
THEOLOGY   David F. Ford
THE TUDORS   John Guy
TWENTIETH-CENTURY
   BRITAIN   Kenneth O. Morgan
WITTGENSTEIN   A. C. Grayling
WORLD MUSIC   Philip Bohlman

Available soon:

AFRICAN HISTORY
  John Parker and Richard Rathbone
THE BRAIN   Michael O'Shea
BUDDHIST ETHICS
  Damien Keown
CHAOS   Leonard Smith
CHRISTIANITY   Linda Woodhead
CITIZENSHIP   Richard Bellamy
CLASSICAL ARCHITECTURE
  Robert Tavernor
CLONING   Arlene Judith Klotzko
CONTEMPORARY ART
  Julian Stallabrass
THE CRUSADES
  Christopher Tyerman
DERRIDA   Simon Glendinning
DESIGN   John Heskett
DINOSAURS   David Norman
DREAMING   J. Allan Hobson
ECONOMICS   Partha Dasgupta
THE END OF THE WORLD
  Bill McGuire
EXISTENTIALISM   Thomas Flynn
THE FIRST WORLD WAR
  Michael Howard
FUNDAMENTALISM
  Malise Ruthven
HABERMAS   Gordon Finlayson

HIROSHIMA   B. R. Tomlinson
HUMAN EVOLUTION
  Bernard Wood
INTERNATIONAL RELATIONS
  Paul Wilkinson
JAZZ   Brian Morton
MANDELA   Tom Lodge
MEDICAL ETHICS
  Tony Hope
THE MIND   Martin Davies
NATIONALISM
  Steven Grosby
PERCEPTION   Richard Gregory
PHILOSOPHY OF RELIGION
  Jack Copeland and Diane Proudfoot
PHOTOGRAPHY
  Steve Edwards
THE RAJ   Denis Judd
THE RENAISSANCE
  Jerry Brotton
RENAISSANCE ART
  Geraldine Johnson
SARTRE   Christina Howells
THE SPANISH CIVIL WAR
  Helen Graham
TRAGEDY   Adrian Poole
THE TWENTIETH CENTURY
  Martin Conway

For more information visit our web site

www.oup.co.uk/vsi

Ian Shaw

ANCIENT EGYPT

A Very Short Introduction

OXFORD
UNIVERSITY PRESS

OXFORD
UNIVERSITY PRESS

Great Clarendon Street, Oxford OX2 6DP

Oxford University Press is a department of the University of Oxford.
It furthers the University's objective of excellence in research, scholarship,
and education by publishing worldwide in

Oxford New York

Auckland Bangkok Buenos Aires Cape Town Chennai
Dar es Salaam Delhi Hong Kong Istanbul Karachi Kolkata
Kuala Lumpur Madrid Melbourne Mexico City Mumbai Nairobi
São Paulo Shanghai Taipei Tokyo Toronto

Oxford is a registered trade mark of Oxford University Press
in the UK and in certain other countries

Published in the United States
by Oxford University Press Inc., New York

© Ian Shaw 2004

The moral rights of the author have been asserted

Database right Oxford University Press (maker)

First published as a very short Introduction 2004

British Library Cataloguing in Publication Data

Data available

Library of Congress Cataloging in Publication Data

Shaw, Ian, 1961
Ancient Egypt : a very short introduction / Ian Shaw p.cm
Includes bibliographical references and index
1. Egypt—Civilization—To 332 B.C. Egypt—antiquities.
3. Egyptology. I. Title. II. Series
DT61.S57 2004 932—dc22—2004050066

ISBN 13: 978-0-19-285419-3
ISBN 10: 0-19-285419-4

3 5 7 9 10 8 6 4

Typeset by RefineCatch Ltd, Bungay Suffolk
Printed in Great Britain by
TJ International Ltd., Padstow, Cornwall

For my parents

Contents

Preface   xi

Acknowledgements   xiii

List of illustrations   xiv

1   Introduction: the story so far   1

2   Discovering and inventing: constructing ancient Egypt   29

3   History: building chronologies and writing histories   48

4   Writing: the origins and implications of hieroglyphs   72

5   Kingship: stereotyping and the 'oriental despot'   82

6   Identity: issues of ethnicity, race, and gender   101

7   Death: mummification, dismemberment, and the cult of Osiris   113

8   Religion: Egyptian gods and temples   126

9   Egyptomania: the recycling and reinventing of Egypt's icons and images   137

References   161

Further reading   166

Useful websites 175

Glossary 178

Timeline 183

Index 185

Preface

In the temple of the goddess Isis on the island of Philae, a few miles to the south of the city of Aswan, one wall bears a brief hieroglyphic inscription. Its significance is not in its content or meaning but purely its date – it was written on 24 August AD 394, and as far as we know it was the last time that the hieroglyphic script was used. The *language* of ancient Egypt survived considerably longer (Philae temple also contains the last graffiti in the more cursive 'demotic' script, dating to 2 December AD 452), and in a sense it still exists in fossilized form in the liturgical texts of the modern Coptic church. Nevertheless, it was around the end of the 4th century AD that the knowledge and use of hieroglyphs effectively vanished, and until the decipherment of hieroglyphs by Jean-François Champollion in 1822, the written world of the Egyptians was unknown, and scholars were almost entirely reliant on the accounts left by Greek and Roman authors, or the sections of the Bible story in which Egypt features. Classical and biblical images of Egypt therefore dominated the emerging subject of Egyptology until almost the end of the 19th century.

More than 180 years after Champollion's breakthrough, the study of ancient Egypt has influenced and permeated a vast number of contemporary issues, from linguistics and 'Afrocentrism', to religious cults and bizarre theories involving extraterrestrials. This book combines discussion of the archaeological and historical study of ancient Egypt with appraisal of the impact of Egypt – and its many icons – on past and present Western society and thought. It is intended both to give the reader a sense of some of the crucial issues that dominate the modern study of ancient Egypt, and also to attempt to discuss some of the reasons why the culture of the Egyptians is still so appealing and fascinating to us.

Much of the discussion in this Very Short Introduction focuses, initially at least, on the 'Narmer Palette' (*c.*3100 BC), outlining its significance with regard to our understanding of early Egyptian culture. Most of the chapters take different aspects of the palette as starting points for consideration of key factors in Egyptology, such as history, writing, religion, and funerary beliefs. Within this structure, current academic Egyptological ideas and discoveries are occasionally compared and contrasted with more populist and commercial viewpoints, including Egypt's widespread exploitation by modern mass media.

Acknowledgements

I would like to thank George Miller for commissioning this book for the Very Short Introduction series, and Emily Jolliffe for making sure that it was written. I would also like to thank Sandra Assersohn for undertaking her usual very efficient work on the illustrations. I am very grateful to Sara Roberts for informing me about Little Warsaw's 'Body of Nefertiti', and to Dr Paul Nicholson for reading through the text. Finally, as usual, most gratitude goes to my family (Ann, Nia, and Elin) who provided both encouragement and distraction when needed.

List of illustrations

1a Front view of the Narmer
   Palette *c.*3000 BC   2
   Egyptian Museum, Cairo. Photo:
   © Jürgen Liepe

1b Back view of the Narmer
   Palette *c.*3000 BC   3
   Egyptian Museum, Cairo. Photo:
   © Jürgen Liepe

2 Line-drawing of Lintel 8
   at Yaxchilan (Chiapas,
   Mexico) *c.* AD 755   8
   Drawing by Ian Graham, Corpus
   of Maya Hieroglyptic
   Inscriptions (Peabody Museum
   Press), fig. V3, courtesy of the
   Peabody Museum of Archaeology
   and Ethnology, Harvard
   University, © President and
   Fellows of Harvard College

3 Illustration from *The
   Panorama of Egypt and
   Nubia*, published in
   1838   21

4 The major sites in
   Egypt and Nubia   22

5 Plan of Hierakonpolis 31
   Original drawing by Barry Kemp
   (after Quibell and Green, 1902,
   pl. LXXII), *Ancient Egypt:
   Anatomy of a Civilisation*
   (Routledge, 1989), fig. 25

6 Satirical reporting of the
   discovery of the tomb
   of Maya at Saqqara
   (*Punch*, 26 Feb.
   1986)   33
   Reproduced with permission of
   Punch Ltd

7 21st-century fieldwork in
   Egypt   41
   © Saqqara Geophysical
   Survey Project

8 The 'Narmer mace-head'
   *c.*3000 BC   51
   Ashmolean Museum, Oxford.
   Photo: © Barbara Ibronyi

9   The 'king-list' from the
    tomb of the priest
    Amenmes at Thebes
    *c.*1300 BC   61
    Original drawing by Barry Kemp
    (after Foucart, 1935, pl. XIIB),
    *Ancient Egypt: Anatomy of a
    Civilisation* (Routledge, 1989),
    fig. 4

10 The unfinished temple at
    Qasr el-Sagha   65
    © Ian Shaw

11 Labels from tomb U-j at
    Abydos *c.*3200 BC   77
    © German Institute of
    Archaeology, Cairo

12 Faience chalice from Tuna
    el-Gebel, 22nd Dynasty,
    *c.*925 BC   83
    © Myers Museum, Eton
    College (ECM 1583)

13 Gneiss statue of Khafra
    from Giza, 4th Dynasty,
    *c.*2500 BC   84
    Egyptian Museum, Cairo. Photo:
    © Jürgen Liepe

14 Granite sphinx of
    Amenemhat III from
    Tanis, 12th Dynasty,
    *c.*1820 BC   86
    Egyptian Museum, Cairo. Photo:
    © Jürgen Liepe

15 Scene in a Deir el-Medina
    tomb-chapel 20th
    Dynasty, *c.*1160 BC   109
    © akg-images, London/Erich
    Lessing

16 The mummified head of
    Seti I, 19th Dynasty,
    *c.*1300 BC   116
    (Egyptian Museum, Cairo)

17 Limestone ostracon 19th
    Dynasty, *c.*1200 BC   128
    © British Museum, London

18 Predynastic female
    figurine with upraised
    arms, *c.*3500 BC   130
    © Brooklyn Museum of Art, New
    York, Charles Edwin Wilbour
    Fund (07.447.505)

19 Professor Edouard Naville
    directing excavations at
    Tell Basta in 1886.   140
    © The Egypt Exploration
    Society

20 The bust of Queen
    Nefertiti *c.*1350 BC   150
    Egyptian Museum, Berlin. Photo:
    © akg-images, London/Gert
    Schütz

21   Elizabeth Taylor as
      Cleopatra and Richard
      Burton as Mark Antony in
      a scene from the 1963

      film, *Antony and
      Cleopatra*   155
      © Twentieth Century
      Fox/Ronald Grant Archive

Chapter 1
Introduction: the story so far

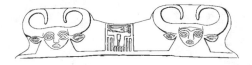

In 1898 the British Egyptologists James Quibell and Frederick Green uncovered a slab of greenish-grey slate-like stone in the ruins of an early temple at the Upper Egyptian site of Hierakonpolis. This was not a find which, like Tutankhamun's tomb 24 years later, would bring the world's journalists racing to the scene, but its discoverers were almost immediately aware of its importance. Like the Rosetta Stone, this carved slab – the Narmer Palette – would have powerful repercussions for the study of ancient Egypt, spreading far beyond its immediate significance at Hierakonpolis. For the next century or so, this object would be variously interpreted by Egyptologists attempting to solve numerous different problems, from the political origins of the Egyptian state to the nature of Egyptian art and writing. No single object can necessarily typify entire culture, but the Narmer Palette is one of a few surviving artefacts from the Nile Valley that are so iconic and so rich in information that they can act as microcosms of certain aspects of ancient Egyptian culture as a whole.

1a. Front view of the Narmer Palette, c.3000 BC.

1b. Back view of the Narmer Palette, *c.*3000 BC.

The Narmer Palette

The palette is one of the first exhibits to be encountered by visitors to the Egyptian Museum in Cairo. It is a shield-shaped slab of greenish stone, 63 cm high, with carved low-relief decoration on both faces, and it is usually dated to the final century of the 4th millennium BC. On the front, there is a depiction of intertwined long-necked lions ('serpopards') held on leashes by two bearded men. Symmetrical pairs of 'tamed' beasts such as these seem to be adapted from early Mesopotamian, perhaps Elamite, iconography, but in an Egyptian context, they may specifically represent the enforced unification of the two halves of the country, which is a theme in Egyptian art and texts throughout the pharaonic period.

The circle formed by the entwining necks of the serpopards ingeniously creates the depression or saucer in which pigments for eye-paint might have been crushed (the original purpose of these palettes), but it is unclear whether such significant ceremonial artefacts as the Narmer Palette were ever actually used for this function. Highly charged ritual objects such as these perhaps transcended the supposed function of the thing itself, as they took on the role of offerings dedicated to the Hierakonpolis temple. On other ceremonial palettes of similar type, the circular depression can have the unwanted effect of interrupting the smooth flow of the scenes depicted – compare for instance the 'Two-dog Palette', also excavated by Quibell and Green at Hierakonpolis, where there are once again two long-necked lions on the front, but the depression simply sits between the necks rather than being created by them (or the 'Battlefield Palette', where the depression interrupts a row of captives).

In the top register on the front of the palette, above the two serpopards, the artist has carved the striding bearded figure of an early Egyptian ruler, probably identified as a man called Narmer, judging by the hieroglyphs both in front of him and in the *serekh* frame in the centre of the top of the palette, between the two cow's heads. He is shown in the so-called Red Crown, which is first attested on a potsherd dating to the Naqada I period (4000–3500 BC) and eventually became connected with the control of Lower Egypt (but whether it had yet developed this association in the time of Naqada I or even Narmer is uncertain). He is also carrying a mace and a flail, and wearing a tunic tied over his left shoulder, with a bull's tail hanging from the waist.

The king is taking part in a procession with six other people, including two figures about half his size, who are behind and in front of him on the palette, but are perhaps intended to be regarded as walking on either side of him in reality. These two men, both clean-shaven, evidently represent high officials. The one to the left is evidently a sandal-bearer, since he carries a pair of sandals in one hand and and a small vessel in the other, while a pectoral, or perhaps royal seal, is tied around his neck by a cord. A single hieroglyph in a rectangular frame or box is placed behind and above his head; this sign, probably being a representation of a reed float (but of uncertain meaning in this context), is usually rendered phonetically as *db3*. He also has two different signs in front of his head, apparently a superimposed rosette sign and the *ḥm* sign that later came to have several meanings, including 'servant'. The official to the right is represented at a slightly larger scale, and is shown wearing a wig and a leopard-skin costume, as well as possibly writing equipment slung around his neck. He may be identified by two hieroglyphs above his head spelling the word *tt̠*, probably an early version of the word for vizier.

The king and these two officials, along with four smaller standard-bearers (all but one of whom are shown bearded), are evidently reviewing the decapitated bodies of ten of their enemies, who are laid out on the far right, each with his head between his legs, presumably in the aftermath of a battle or ritual slaughter. The four standards are topped by symbols or totems which are known from later periods, comprising two falcons, one jackal (perhaps the god Wepwawet), and a strange globular item that is clearly the *šdšd* or royal placenta). These standards, taken together, form a group that were later identified as the so-called 'followers of Horus' (or 'the gods who follow Horus') and had strong associations with the celebration of a royal jubilee or funeral. Above the corpses are four signs or images: a door, a falcon, a boat with high prow and stern, and a falcon holding a harpoon.

On the other side of the palette is a much larger, muscular striding figure of Narmer, this time shown wearing the conical White Crown of Upper Egypt along with the same tunic tied over his left shoulder and the bull's tail hanging from his waist, as well as fringes ending in cow's heads. This time he is accompanied only by the sandal-bearer (behind him, or to one side), as he smites a foreigner with a pear-shaped mace held up above his head (but held slightly oddly, halfway up the handle). The sandal-bearer is again shown at just under half the size of the king (although the ruler's tall crown makes him tower even more over the rest of the figures in the scene), and once more he has the rosette and *ḥm* signs by his head. The king is gripping the hair of the captive (whose facial features seem Egyptian rather than Libyan or Asiatic), and the latter has two ideograms floating to the right of his head. These two small images are presumed by most Egyptologists to be the early hieroglyphs for 'harpoon' (*w'*) and 'lake' (*š*), which would either phonetically spell out the foreign name 'Wash', or refer to someone whose name, title, or even place of origin was actually 'Harpoon (lake)'. It seems likely that the falcon holding a harpoon, depicted as one of the group of enigmatic signs above the decapitated bodies on the front of the palette (see above) is also communicating the idea of the defeat of Wash/Harpoon by the king in the guise of the Horus-falcon.

In front of the king, and above the captive, the falcon-god Horus hovers, holding a schematically rendered captive by a rope attached to the man's nose. This captive has six papyri protruding from his back, and it has been suggested that this identifies the rebus as '6,000 captives', on the basis that each of the papyrus plants already signifies the number 1,000 as they later would in the pharaonic period. An alternative reading is that this group of plants is an iconographical reference to the homeland of the captive, which might have been the papyrus-filled land of northern Egypt. It is possible that the 'harpoon' and 'lake' signs may be intended to refer to the king's captive as well as to the one held by the falcon, so that both may actually be the same person/people. In the lowest section of this side of the palette are two prone naked human figures, who are presumably also intended to be either captives or dead enemies. Each of these has a sign to the left of his face and both of their bodies are twisted so that their faces are pointing leftwards, i.e. in the same direction as the two captives above (and in the opposite direction to the king and the sandal-bearer).

The visual appearance and the very complex content of the Narmer Palette's decoration have been the subject of constant discussion ever since its discovery. The style of the images and the identification of the king as Narmer demonstrate that it was created at the end of the 4th millennium BC, when many of the most distinctive elements of Egyptian culture were emerging. The images already incorporate a number of highly characteristic features of pharaonic art, such as the arrangement of the picture into a series of horizontal 'registers', the semi-diagrammatic depiction of people and animals as a combination of frontal and sideways elements, and the use of size as a means of indicating each individual's relative importance. The latter is very much the iconography of power.

In a cross-cultural study of the palette, the Canadian archaeologist, Bruce Trigger, points out that the specific 'Egyptianness' of the smiting scene can be counterbalanced by various aspects of the iconography that seem to be universal. Pointing out the obvious contrast between the king's elaborate regalia and his virtually naked victim, he cites the Victory Stele of Eannatum (c.2560 BC), on which the god Ningirsu wields a mace over a group of naked enemies trapped in a net. He also notes the tradition among North American Iroquoians of stripping captured warriors of some of their clothing and ornamentation, and the Akkadian depictions of 'naked, fettered

2. **Lintel 8 at Yaxchilan showing a Maya act of capture, *c.*AD 755.**

captives'. He makes a fascinating comparison with a Maya scene on a carved lintel from Yaxchilan, showing a ruler called Bird-Jaguar capturing two of his enemies (*c.*AD 755). In the Maya scene, the richly clothed triumphant warriors contrast with the semi-naked defeated rulers, one of whom is held by his hair. As Trigger concludes,

> Although the scene on the Narmer palette does not necessarily depict the capture in battle of an adversary, the psychological affinities between these two representations are very close, notwithstanding their having evolved wholly independently of one another, in different hemispheres, and far removed in time.

This comment might be applied in some respects to Egyptian culture as a whole, where we find ourselves constantly veering between the thought that 'they're just like us' to the alternative view that they are also very peculiarly and distinctively Egyptian. As Barry Kemp says, in *Ancient Egypt: Anatomy of a Civilisation* (much recommended as a fairly long introduction to ancient Egypt),

> We can, as it were, walk in and out of [the Egyptians'] thought processes without being too aware of their strangeness because their language and images are a part of the process by which, from birth, we in the west classify reality . . . My ancient Egypt is very much an imagined world, though I hope that it cannot too readily be shown to be untrue to the original ancient sources.

In another intriguing Egyptological book, *ReMembering Osiris*, Tom Hare makes a similar point:

> Ancient Egypt is dead. No-one can claim a natural ethnic or linguistic privilege with it. But the extraordinary remoteness of its 'timelessness' and all the potency of nostalgia raise Egypt from the dead, despite the erosion of tens of centuries and the most assiduous defacements and depredations of Romans, Copts and Muslims, Imperial soldiers, philologists, civic engineers, and tourists. Despite all this, Egypt remains.

If the attraction of ancient Egyptian culture is its combination of exotica and familiarity, the role of the Egyptologist seems to be to use the available archaeological, visual, and textual sources to distinguish between, on the one hand, aspects of life that are culturally specific either to ourselves or to the ancient Egyptians and, on the other, what Kemp describes as 'a core which has remained fixed and basic since the appearance of the first states in the ancient world'. This is of course not the only reason for studying the civilization of ancient Egypt, although it is this mindset that constantly challenges us to view Egypt not in isolation but as one of many human cultural responses to particular environmental and historical conditions.

What is ancient Egypt?

The earliest 'Egyptians' (if we can call them this before Egypt existed) appeared in Palaeolithic north-eastern Africa in *c.*400,000 BC, but they did not begin to focus their encampments near the River Nile until the onset of a drier climate in about 25,000 BC, at which time the eastern and western deserts formed. During the Mesolithic period (*c.*10,000–5000 BC) a number of semi-nomadic cultures inhabited the immediate area of the Nile Valley, relying on hunting and fishing for their subsistence. Finally a gradual moistening of the climate in about 6000 BC encouraged the development of more settled Neolithic communities along the Nile, primarily relying on animal and plant domestication.

By the beginning of the 4th millennium BC, a distinctive civilization had emerged at the northern end of the Nile Valley. Rainfall was (and still is) very low throughout the region, so the rich agricultural land of Egypt (which the ancient Egyptians called Kemet: 'black land') was watered by the so-called 'inundation', the apparently miraculous annual flooding of the river, which deposited new layers of fertile silt along the riverbanks. The strips of cultivated land vary in thickness on either side, as the river meanders northwards. The River Nile, running northwards from its source in East Africa to the Mediterranean coast, is therefore the single most important element in the geography of Egypt. It divides the country into two sections: first Upper Egypt, the southern part, consisting of the land from Wadi Halfa to Cairo, and secondly Lower Egypt, essentially comprising the northern region where the Nile fans out into several branches, forming a large and fertile delta, before disgorging into the Mediterranean. The ancient Egyptians called their country Kemet (referring to the black fertile soil), in contrast to the surrounding Deshret ('red land' or desert). Within this simple and curiously symmetrical geographical setting there developed a sophisticated culture, many aspects of which invariably shared these same qualities of balance and harmony.

The archaeology of pharaonic Egypt spans three millennia (*c*.3100–332 BC) and encompasses a diverse body of artefacts, architecture, texts, and organic remains. Museums throughout the world contain millions of Egyptian antiquities, and an even greater number of remains are still *in situ* in the Nile Valley and the Delta, ranging from temples, tombs, and cities to remote rock inscriptions carved on crags in the Libyan Desert, the Eastern Desert, or the Sinai peninsula. Three principal factors have facilitated the survival of an unusual wealth of detail concerning pharaonic Egypt: first, an elite group's penchant for grandiose and elaborate funerary arrangements, secondly, suitably arid conditions of preservation, and finally the use of writing on a wide variety of media.

The history of the rediscovery of pharaonic Egypt is in many respects the same as that of any other ancient civilization, in that centuries of ignorance and plundering were gradually replaced by the more enlightened approaches of late 19th-century and 20th-century scholars. Within this broad trend, however, various specific aspects of Egyptology, such as epigraphy, excavation, philology, and anthropology, have progressed at very different rates.

Greek and Roman views of Egypt

The first people from outside Egypt to take it upon themselves to study the Egyptians as a unique and fascinating anthropological phenomenon were the ancient Greeks. Although archaeological evidence in Egypt and elsewhere shows that there were commercial contacts between Egyptians and Greeks from at least the late 3rd millennium BC, it was recruitment of large numbers of Greek mercenary soldiers by the 26th-Dynasty ruler Psamtek I, in the 7th century BC, that probably marked the beginning of full-scale contact between the two civilizations.

Apart from Homer's many references to Egypt in the *Iliad*, some of the first written evidence for Greek interest in Egypt derives from their early study of the geography of the world as a whole. In the 6th century BC, Thales of Miletus wrote a description of the Nile inundation, which he suggested was caused by winds blowing from the north in the summer, thus preventing the river from reaching the Mediterranean. At around the same time, Anaximander produced the first scientifically based map of the surface of the earth; according to Herodotus, a copper tablet reproducing Anaximander's map included 'the whole circuit of the earth and all the sea and rivers', so we can probably assume that it included the Nile Valley.

Between the 5th century BC and the 2nd century AD, numerous Greek and Roman scholars visited Egypt, and the accounts that they gave of their visits provide our first real verbal and intellectual view of Egypt from the outside. Sadly, however, the works of many ancient writers on Egypt have not survived, and one major reason for this was the burning of the library at Alexandria in 47 BC and then again in AD 391, when 700,000 works, including Manetho's 36-volume history of Egypt (see Chapter 3 below), were lost.

The first Greek geographer who is definitely known to have visited Egypt was Hecataeus of Miletus, who travelled as far south as Thebes in about 500 BC. He wrote a treatise called the *Periodos* ('description'), which was the first systematic account of the geography of the world. Only fragments of this work have survived, but it clearly included a detailed description of Egypt, because Stephanus of Byzantium (*c*.AD 600) cites 15 Egyptian town-names from it.

The best-known, and most informative, ancient Greek visitor to Egypt was of course Herodotus of Halicarnassus, the traveller and historian. His nine volumes of *Histories* were written between 430 and 425 BC, and the second book is entirely devoted to Egypt. Herodotus is the earliest major textual source of information on mummification and other ancient Egyptian religious and funerary customs, and he attracted numerous later imitators, including Strabo and Diodorus Siculus. His travels in Egypt may have extended as far south as Aswan, but he gives no detailed account of Thebes, concentrating mainly on places in Lower Egypt. He seems to have relied mainly on rather low-ranking Egyptian priests for his evidence, but his astute observations included the identification of the pyramids as royal burial places. Herodotus not only provides a great deal of ethnographic information on 5th-century Egypt, but also gives us a version of Egyptian history for about 200 years of the Late Period, from the reign of Psamtek I, *c*.650 to the date that Herodotus visited Egypt, *c*.450 (by which time Egypt had become a satrapy in the Persian Empire). Occasionally archaeological work has shown Herodotus' descriptions to be surprisingly accurate, as in the case of Tell Basta, the site of the temple and town of Bubastis, in the eastern Nile Delta, about 80 km to the north-east of Cairo. In 1887–9, Edouard Naville's excavation of the main monument at the site, the red granite temple of the cat-goddess Bastet, confirmed many of the architectural details of the Greek historian's report.

Herodotus' description of Egypt has been described by the British Egyptologist Alan Lloyd as 'our only consecutive account of Egyptian history between 664 and 525 BC and, for all its faults, it continues to provide the bedrock on which all modern work on the period is based'. Lloyd makes the point that native Egyptian texts of the 5th century BC, although quite extensive, are to a large extent full of stereotyped, obsolescent material that cannot be regarded as reliable. Herodotus, however, is not without his own problems, and according to Lloyd, he 'presents a view of Egypt's past which shows no genuine understanding of Egyptian history. Everything has been uncompromisingly customized for Greek consumption and cast unequivocally into a Greek mold.' As long ago as 1887, it was demonstrated by the German philologist Herman Diels that Herodotus was extensively plagiarizing the work of his illustrious predecessor Hecataeus, especially in the geographical and ethnographic sections of his Egyptian volume. It has consequently been argued that Hecataeus ought to have at least some of the credit for developing the basic intellectual framework that characterized Herodotus and most later Greek authors writing about Egypt.

The next Greek to write extensively on Egypt from personal experience was another Hecataeus (*c*.320–300 BC), this time a philosopher and historian born in the Thracian town of Abdera. He was the author of many books, including one, probably called *Concerning the Egyptians* (*Aegyptiaca*), which was apparently based on the time he spent in Egypt in the employ of Ptolemy I, the founder of the Ptolemaic dynasty. Although he almost certainly travelled up the Nile with Ptolemy, his writings include numerous extracts plagiarized from Herodotus. Hecataeus was a pupil of the sceptic Pyrrho, and although only fragments of his works have survived, he is quoted by a number of authors, including Diodorus Siculus. His book on Egypt is the earliest surviving Greek history to mention the Jews. He also provides a good indication of Greeks' views of the ancient Egyptian political system in the early Ptolemaic period, although his view of Egyptian kingship seems unfortunately to be way off the mark, including the suggestion that,

in general the priests are the first to deliberate on the most important matters, and are always at the king's side, sometimes as his helpers, sometimes as proposers of measures and teachers; and they also forecast future events by astrology and divination, and make known to him those acts recorded in the sacred books which can be of assistance.

It has been argued that Hecataeus's view of Ptolemaic kingship was biased by two factors: first, the use of priests and priestly documents as sources, and second, the tendency of Greek authors to add their own ideas into descriptions of 'oriental' customs.

Not all Greeks were in Egypt to research books, some of them were in the Nile Valley for commercial or military reasons (or just passing through), and these individuals have left behind some of the earliest tourist and 'pilgrimage' graffiti on the sights and monuments that they visited. One of the best collections of this kind of graffiti is on the northernmost of the Colossi of Memnon, two colossal statues that stand in front of the remains of Amenhotep III's mortuary temple on the west bank at Thebes (the Greeks knew the statue as the 'vocal Memnon', interpreting the unusual whistling noise it made each morning as the Homeric character Memnon singing to his mother Eos, goddess of the dawn). Even at the remote temples of Ramesses II down at Abu Simbel in Nubia there are graffiti left by Carian, Greek, and Phoenician soldiers who formed part of Psamtek II's expedition against the Kushites in the early 6th century BC. The Greek historian Strabo, who spent several years at Alexandria in the late first century BC, discusses several of the Theban monuments, including the Colossi and the New Kingdom rock-tombs. Although not generally as informative as the work of Herodotus, and considerably more prone to patronizing remarks concerning Egyptian culture, Strabo's *Geography* is nevertheless a valuable record of Egypt in the 1st century BC.

Herodotus and his successors not only provide us with information about Egypt in the Late Period and Greco-Roman times, they also help to give us a sense of the intellectual and spiritual concerns of Egyptians. Although the Greek and Roman writers frequently seem to have been wrong in their assessment of the Egyptians' religion and philosophy, their reactions often involve the same kind of complex mixture of responses that are evoked in many modern researchers. Thus for instance Lucian, a Roman satirist in the 1st century AD, who, at one stage in his career, served on the staff of the prefect of Egypt, wrote a dialogue between the gods Momos and Zeus in which he conveys a very precise sense of the Romans' simultaneous mockery and sneaking admiration for Egyptian religious customs. Momos asks:

'You there, you dog-faced, linen-vested Egyptian, who do you think you are, my good man, and how do you consider yourself to be a god with that bark of yours? ... I am ashamed to mention ibises and apes and goats and other far more ludicrous creatures who have been smuggled out of Egypt into heaven, goodness knows how. How can you bear, gods, to see them worshipped on equal terms, or even better, with yourselves? And you, Zeus, how can you put up with it when they stick a ram's horns on to you?'

Zeus, however, replies,

'These things you say about the Egyptians are truly shocking. Nevertheless, Momos, the majority of them have mystic significance and it is quite wrong for one who is not an initiate to mock them.'

The Bible and Egypt

There can be no doubting the presence of Greeks and Romans in Egypt, but attempts to correlate biblical narratives with the Egyptian textual and archaeological record have always been distinctly problematic. Most scholars' efforts to assign precise dates to biblical episodes involving Egypt tend to be thwarted by the uncertainty of the chronological background of the Old Testament. It also seems likely that many events of great significance to the Israelites cannot be assumed to have had the same importance for the ancient Egyptians, therefore there is no guarantee of any independent Egyptian record having been made, let alone being one of the very small proportion of texts that have actually survived.

Definite datable references to Egypt do not seem to appear in the Bible until the 1st millennium BC, when there are a number of specific allusions to the Egyptians, particularly in connection with battles against the Assyrians and Persians. It may have been during the reign of the 22nd-Dynasty ruler 'Osorkon the elder' (984–978) that Hadad the Edomite, stayed in Egypt. A later 22nd-Dynasty ruler Shoshenq I (945–924) is almost certainly the biblical Shishak, who is said to have pillaged Jerusalem and the temple of Solomon in 925. About two centuries later, the Egyptian prince Tefnakht of Sais, is said to have been contacted by Hosea, the ruler of Samaria, when he was looking for military aid in his struggles against an Assyrian invasion.

However, these very specific references to named rulers are the exception, and in general provable links between ancient Egypt and the Old Testament narrative are controversial and heavily debated. Since most of the events described in the Bible occurred several hundred years before the time that they were written down, it is extremely difficult to know when they are factual historical accounts and when they are purely allegorical or rhetorical in nature. Further potential problems occur because of anachronistic Egyptian names, places, or cultural phenomena that may belong not to the time when the events are supposed to have happened, but to later periods when the texts were actually written down. This may be the case, for instance, with the story of Joseph, which is usually assumed to have taken place in the New Kingdom (1550–1070) but contains certain details that tie in much more with the political situation of the Saite period (664–525).

Probably the most frequently discussed biblical link with Egypt is the Exodus narrative. There is a popular assumption that Ramesses II (whose overall reputation is discussed in Chapter 5) was the pharaoh involved in the expulsion of the Israelites from Egypt. The evidence linking Ramesses specifically with the Exodus story is fairly slim, hinging partly on the fact that the city where the enslaved Israelites were supposed to have laboured was Piramesse, the site founded by Ramesses and his father in the eastern Delta. It has also been pointed out that Ramesses' eldest son, Amunherkhepeshef appears to vanish from the records fairly early in his father's reign, leading some scholars to suggest that he might have died young and thus might be a theoretical candidate for pharaoh's slaughtered 'firstborn' in the Exodus narrative. However, Farouk Gomaa argues that this son might simply have changed his name to Amunherwenemef or Sethherkhepeshef, both of which continue to appear in texts until fairly late in Ramesses' reign. If Gomaa is correct, this particular son would therefore still be alive in the 40th year of Ramesses II's reign, thus suggesting that he was perhaps in his fifties when he died, making him a much less plausible candidate for the slaughtered firstborn.

Sadly Gomaa was about half a century too late to prevent Cecil B. DeMille from casting Ramesses as the villain in his celebrated silent movie *The Ten Commandments* (1923). The same excuse cannot apply to the 1990s Dreamworks Exodus-set animation, *Prince of Egypt*, in which Ramesses was once again in the hot seat, and the script-writers were evidently unaware of Gomaa's careful arguments.

Some Egyptologists have suggested that the 'pharaoh' of the Exodus was actually Ramesses' son and successor Merenptah, partly on the basis of a 'victory stele' from the latter's reign that is the earliest document of any kind to mention Israel. Dating to the fifth year of his reign (*c.*1208), it consists of a series of hymns celebrating Merenptah's victories over various foreign enemies. Among the Palestinian enemies is the word Israel, significantly accompanied by a hieroglyph that indicates a people rather than a town or geographical area:

> Plundered is Canaan with every evil; carried off is Ashkelon; seized upon is Gezer; Yanoam is made as that which does not exist; Israel is laid waste, his seed is not; Hurru has become a widow for Egypt. All lands together, they are pacified.

However, as this translated extract shows, the stele actually tells us very little about the origins or nature of Israel, and certainly makes no reference to the presence of Israelites in Egypt, let alone their expulsion. As John Laughlin puts it, rather emphatically,

> Some textual evidence, such as the Papyrus Anastasi V ... might allow one to hypothesise that a few Egyptian slaves could have slipped out of Egypt from time to time, but all of the known Egyptian texts put together do not even remotely hint at an 'Exodus' as described in the Bible. The Merenptah stele is simply irrelevant to this question.

More recently, even Queen Hatshepsut, in the early 18th Dynasty, has emerged as a possible contender for the Exodus pharaoh, on the somewhat dubious grounds that the parting of the waters of the Red Sea could then be explained as a result of the volcanic eruption on the island of Santorini in the Aegean (although most estimates of the date of this eruption now set it at *c.*1620, about 150 years before her reign). However, the Canadian Egyptologist, Donald Redford, argues more radically that the Exodus account is simply a mishmash of stories which probably originated in distant memories of the expulsion of the Hyksos (the Asiatic kings who ruled northern Egypt during the Second Intermediate Period). In *Moses the Egyptian*, Jan Assmann suggests that it represents not only a folk memory of the end of the Hyksos period, when Egypt expelled Asiatic rulers from northern Egypt, but perhaps also a kind of mythologization of the so-called 'heretical' Amarna period (for more on which, see Chapter 9). He concludes that the Exodus story is ultimately to be regarded as a convenient use of such folk tales to allow the Israelites to define themselves as a distinct nation: 'Egypt's role in the Exodus story is not historical but mythical: it helps define the very identity of those who tell the story.'

An intriguing direct literary (and perhaps religious) link between Egypt and the Bible is Psalm 104, which has strong similarities with a hymn to the Aten, the god of the sun-disc. This hymn is said to have been composed by the pharaoh Akhenaten, who is credited with transforming Egyptian religion into a single cult considered by some to be monotheistic. Attempts have occasionally been made to equate Akhenaten with Moses (including Sigmund Freud no less, who published a book called *Moses and Monotheism*). However, there are no other aspects of this pharaoh's life, or indeed his cult of the Aten, that resemble the biblical account of Moses. The similarities with the psalm probably result only from the fact that the two compositions belong to a common literary heritage – they may even both derive from a common Near Eastern original. The same reason is usually given for the very close parallels that have been observed between a Late Period wisdom text known as the *Instruction of Amenemipet son of Kanakht* and the biblical book of

Proverbs, although it has been suggested by some scholars that the writers of Proverbs may even have been influenced by a text of the *Instruction of Amenemipet* itself.

It is an irony of biblical archaeology that the more we investigate the texts and archaeological remains that link Egypt with the Bible, the less substantial and the less convincing these kinds of connections appear to be. As John Romer observed in *Testament: The Bible and history*: 'Ultimately archaeology can neither "prove" nor "disprove" the Old Testament, only modern theories about what it might mean.' The biblical archaeology of Egypt was perhaps always doomed to be something of a blind alley, but undoubtedly in the early years of Egyptology both classical and biblical writings played the crucial role of familiar routes into an otherwise alien and largely incomprehensible landscape.

The emergence of 'Egyptology'

As with the question of the date at which European antiquarianism was superseded by archaeology, it is not easy to suggest a specific date when the writings of 'early travellers' and the collecting of Egyptian antiquities became transformed into something approaching the modern discipline of Egyptology. Most histories of Egyptian archaeology, however, see the Napoleonic expedition at the beginning of the 19th century as the first systematic attempt to record and describe the standing remains of pharaonic Egypt. The importance of the *Description de l'Egypte* –the multi-volume publication that resulted from the expedition – lay not only in its high standards of draughtsmanship and accuracy but also in the fact that it constituted a continuous and internally consistent appraisal by a single group of scholars, thus providing the first real assessment of ancient Egypt in its entirety.

Despite the scientific aims of Napoleon's 'savants', virtually all 19th-century excavations in Egypt were designed to provide art treasures

3. Illustration from *The Panorama of Egypt and Nubia* (1838).

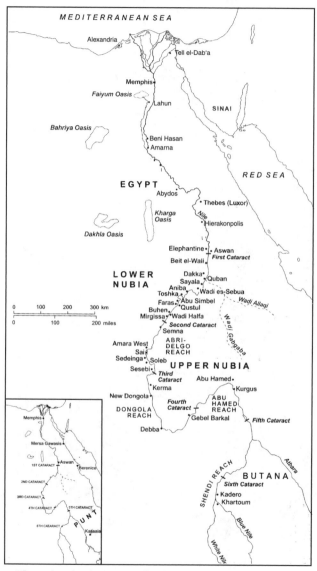

4. The major sites in Egypt and Nubia.

for European and American museums and private collections, since the expeditions' financial support invariably derived from these sources. What is remarkable about the European expeditions to Egypt in the first half of the 19th century is the rapid pace with which new information was acquired, digested, and assimilated into the overall picture of the pharaonic period. In 1838 the French architect Hector Horeau published a 'panorama' of Egypt including an illustration showing the principal monuments of Egypt. The painting took the form of an imaginary view of the meandering course of the River Nile, with Alexandria and the Mediterranean coast in the foreground, and the temple of Isis on the island of Philae in the far distance. This pictorial view of Egypt, already incorporating the basic essentials of Egyptian architecture, from the pyramids at Giza to the temples of eastern and western Thebes, is a good metaphor for the speed with which the bare bones of Egyptology were assembled. As early as the 1830s, Gardner Wilkinson was able to present a wide-ranging and detailed view of ancient Egypt in his *Manners and Customs*. Certainly there were inaccuracies, misconceptions, and omissions in the publications of the mid-19th century, but in many respects the fundamentals were already known, and the last one and a half centuries have arguably been more concerned with filling in the details than breaking new ground.

Between the period of organized plundering undertaken by such men as Giovanni Belzoni and Bernardino Drovetti in the early 19th century and the excavations of Emile Amélineau and Jacques de Morgan in the 1890s, there was surprisingly little development in the techniques employed by Egyptian archaeologists. John Wortham neatly encapsulates this phase in his history of British Egyptology: 'Although archaeologists no longer used dynamite to excavate sites, their techniques remained unrefined'.

Arguably one of the most insidious and retrogressive aspects of 19th-century archaeology in Egypt was the concept of 'clearance', as opposed to scientific excavation. The very word appeared to substantiate the fallacy that the sand simply had to be removed in order to reveal the significant monuments hidden below, thus helping to discourage the proper consideration of stratigraphic excavation and the appreciation of all components of a site – sand, potsherds, mud bricks, and towering stone gateways – as equally important and integral elements of the archaeological record. The use of the term 'clearance' also encouraged the feeling that the antiquities of Egypt simply needed to be exposed and displayed rather than be analysed, interpreted, or reconstructed. From the 1880s onwards, however, the emergence of more scientific approaches gradually hauled Egyptology into a more methodical era.

In the late 19th and early 20th centuries, at a time when scientific methods of fieldwork and analysis were still developing throughout the various branches of archaeology, the innovative methods of two particular Egyptologists, Flinders Petrie and George Reisner, set new standards for the discipline as a whole. This was perhaps the only stage in its history when Egyptian archaeology was at the forefront of the development of methodology, setting the pattern for excavations in Europe and America. Despite differences in their social origins and academic backgrounds, the careers of both Petrie and Reisner were similar in that each was a pioneer but also, more prosaically, each was largely financed by a female benefactor (in Petrie's case, the British novelist Amelia Edwards, and in Reisner's case, the American philanthropist Phoebe Apperson).

Petrie's fieldwork in Egypt and Palestine was innovative primarily because he paid such close attention to every detail of the archaeological deposits that he was excavating, whereas his predecessors and contemporaries (and even some of his successors) concentrated primarily on the unearthing and description of the large monumental features of sites. Whereas other 19th-century 'excavators' tended to clear large tracts of archaeological material relatively indiscriminately, Petrie dug in strategically selected parts of each site, thus building up an overall picture of the remains without destroying the entire site in the process. At Amarna, for instance, he obtained a good overview of a complex urban site in a single season by excavating a range of different types of structure in various parts of the city.

Arriving on the scene some 20 years after Petrie, Reisner was nevertheless equally pioneering in his approach. In some respects he resembled Petrie, in that he worked with an enormous attention to detail, but he also moved the subject on through his recognition that his surveys or excavations needed to be not only undertaken with great care, but also recorded in such meticulous detail that any future researcher would be able to reconstruct both the site and the process by which it was originally examined. Since he died before publishing a great deal of his work (one of the drawbacks of his exceedingly painstaking approach), it was just as well that his results could be interpreted and published by future generations of archaeologists. Part of the secret of his success was his use of genuinely multidisciplinary teams actually in the field, as opposed to submitting material to scientists at some later date, when their context and local significance might have been less clear. At the Predynastic cemetery of Naga ed-Der, for instance, he was accompanied by the anatomist Grafton Elliot Smith, whose detailed observations on the material from cemetery N7000 have provided modern researchers with an extremely reliable anthropological database. It was also Reisner who introduced the systematic use of the section drawing into Egyptian archaeology, some 40 years after such stratigraphic analysis had been pioneered by Giuseppe Fiorelli at Pompeii. All previous excavators in Egypt (including Petrie) had simply used sequences of horizontal plans to describe the various stages in the history of a site.

It has to be admitted, however, that the achievements of Petrie and Reisner were something of an aberration. For most of its history, Egyptology has tended to be extremely conservative, both in overall conceptual terms and with regard to methods of post-excavation analysis and interpretation of archaeological data. Even in the early 1970s there were still relatively few indications that archaeologists working in Egypt and the Near East were embarking on any radical changes in their methods of analysis and interpretation, particularly when compared with the many advances that had been made in prehistory and historical archaeology elsewhere in the world. While mainstream archaeologists such as Lewis Binford, Colin Renfrew, and Michael Schiffer were expanding the theoretical basis of archaeology, most Egyptologists were still preoccupied with the business of pure data-gathering and history-writing.

In Bruce Trigger's *A History of Archaeological Thought*, there are a mere handful of references to Egyptian archaeology: only Flinders Petrie's invention of an early form of seriation known as 'sequence dating' merits a full page or so of discussion. While this may well be a fair assessment of the Egyptological contribution to archaeological *thought*, the excavation of Egyptian sites has, over the last 150 years, provided a steady stream of valuable *data*. The rapidly expanding Egyptian database has provided new insights into the material culture of the pharaonic period, but, perhaps more importantly, it has also made a significant contribution to the creation of a chronological framework for the Mediterranean region. The central role played by Egyptology in the formulation of ancient chronology has lent greater significance to recent attempts to pinpoint flaws in the chronology of the pharaonic period, but the established chronology is now a dense matrix of archaeological and textual details that have proved difficult to unpick and reassemble.

Most of the work accomplished by archaeologists in Egypt between the mid-19th century and the Second World War was characterized by two distinct trends. First, the early work in particular was marked by a resolutely art-historical, object-oriented approach to the excavated data. Secondly, the fieldwork was dominated by a preference for the study of religious and funerary architecture rather than the artefacts and architecture of daily life. Both of these tendencies effectively inhibited the intellectual development of Egyptian archaeology until the 1960s, when two major influences – the study of the prehistory of the Nile Valley and the increased excavation of pharaonic towns – finally began to exert an influence on the subject as a whole.

In an analysis of changing patterns in Egyptological research (see Tables 1 and 2), David O'Connor has demonstrated that the percentage of published archaeological fieldwork devoted to settlements almost doubled from 1924 to 1981. The situation

Table 1: Proportions of published Egyptological work

		1924	1981
Language & texts	based mainly on texts	15.5	19.1
History & religion	based mainly on texts	17.2	10.8
Society & culture	based mainly on texts	3.5	5.5
Art		2.0	4.6
Archaeology (incl. epigraphy & field reports)		33.2	27.2

Table 2: Proportions of types of archaeological fieldwork

Publication	Monumental		Non-monumental		Survey
	Funerary	*Religious*	*Cemetery*	*Settlement*	
1924	34.1	20.7	30.5	13.4	1.0
1981	36.2	13.0	8.7	23.2	15.9
1982	34.6	17.9	11.5	17.9	17.9
1990	27.8	16.7	5.6	44.4	5.6

All details except those for 1990 taken from D. O'Connor, 'Egyptology and Archaeology: An African Perspective', in P. Robertshaw (ed.), *A History of African Archaeology* (London, 1990).

appears to have changed even more dramatically in the 1990s, with the 1989–90 list of Egyptological publications showing no less than 44.4 per cent of fieldwork dealing with settlement remains, and a correspondingly steep decline in the excavation of non-monumental cemeteries. Modern Egyptologists are therefore undoubtedly more 'balanced' and holistic with regard to the types of data that they now study. The next chapter will consider the different types of discovery, analysis, and interpretation of old and new evidence.

Chapter 2

Discovering and inventing: constructing ancient Egypt

The Narmer Palette was discovered about a metre away from a buried collection of ceremonial objects dating to the Late Predynastic and Early Dynastic periods (*c.*3100–2700), including ceremonial cosmetic palettes, mace-heads, and carved ivory figurines. This assemblage of artefacts discovered by Quibell and Green – and described by them as the 'main deposit' – has since proved to be one of the most important sets of evidence for our understanding of the beginnings of the Egyptian state. Unfortunately, because of a lack of accurate published plans and stratigraphic sections from the site, the full significance and the true date of this crucial early find remain unclear. In the vicinity, the excavators also discovered several valuable pieces from somewhat later in Egyptian history, including two unique copper alloy statues of the late Old Kingdom ruler Pepi I (2321–2287) and the golden head of a falcon which is perhaps part of one of the cult statues worshipped in the temple. The mixture of objects of different dates suggests that they comprised a whole series of royal gifts to the temple, but we have no way of knowing whether each piece was brought to the temple in person by a number of rulers from the late Predynastic through to the Old Kingdom, or whether they were all dedicated en masse by a later ruler in the Old or Middle Kingdoms.

Some of Quibell's comments on the excavation of the 'main deposit' and the immediately surrounding area convey a rather honest despair that their techniques were not quite equal to the task:

> Day after day we sat in this hole, scraping away the earth, and trying to disentangle the objects from one another; for they lay in every possible position, each piece in contact with five or six others, interlocking as a handful of matches will, when shaken together and thrown down upon a table.

In *Egypt before the Pharaohs*, the American prehistorian Michael Hoffman summarized just how much of a hash seems to have been made by Quibell and Green (although it would also be a mistake to underestimate the complexity of their task at Hierakonpolis):

> Sadly we do not even know for sure where the most graphic piece of evidence, the Narmer Palette, actually came from. It was evidently found near the Main Deposit but not actually with the other material. From Green's field notes (Quibell kept none!) it seems to have been found a metre or two away, and Green noted in the 1902 publication that it was found in a place directly associated with an apparently Protodynastic level, which would date it to a generation or two before the unification of the Two Lands in 3100 B.C. But two years earlier, in the first report published on Hierakonpolis by Quibell, it was labelled as coming from the Main Deposit proper, a feature that may be as late as the Middle Kingdom (ca. 2130–1785 B.C.).

The particular nature and context of Quibell and Green's discovery of the Narmer Palette at Hierakonpolis highlight the fact that great

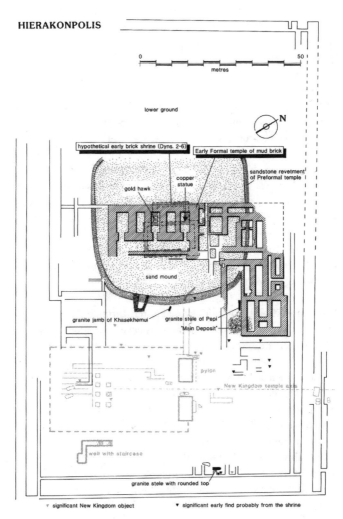

HIERAKONPOLIS

0 _____ 50
metres

lower ground

N

hypothetical early brick shrine (Dyns. 2-6)

Early Formal temple of mud brick

copper statue

gold hawk

sandstone revetment of Preformal temple

sand mound

granite jamb of Khasekhemui

granite stele of Pepi

"Main Deposit"

pylon

New Kingdom temple axis

well with staircase

granite stele with rounded top

▽ significant New Kingdom object   ▼ significant early find probably from the shrine

5. **Plan of Hierakonpolis, showing where the 'Main Deposit' and other objects were found.**

finds can in extreme cases be rendered almost meaningless if their full context is not properly recorded. Even the most meticulous excavation may sometimes run up against interpretive problems, but, conversely, if discoveries are made or published in an unscientific way then there is only the slimmest chance of their full meaning becoming apparent.

Historically, Egyptology is immensely rich in data, and Egyptologists have consequently tended to be data-hungry scholars. A constant succession of fresh discoveries has ensured that the evidence itself has been steadily increasing in quantity and diversity. It is noticeable, however, that archaeological discoveries in Egypt have become such a cliché, in the way that the media respond to them and portray the discoveries and the protagonists, that an issue of *Punch* in 1986 was able to satirize very effectively the breathless and overblown way in which a new find (in this case the tomb of a man called Maya, Tutankhamun's treasurer) is pumped up into a mini-Tutankhamun's tomb, as if the newspaper reports automatically switch into a particularly fossilized and naïve style of reportage when confronted by the glint of hidden treasure.

The subject itself has not progressed purely through discoveries of new data. New theoretical paradigms have been adopted by different generations of Egyptologists, gradually transforming the accepted picture of ancient Egyptian culture. Secondly, new methods, such as innovative excavation techniques or sophisticated methods of scientific analysis, have, at various times, altered our perceptions of the surviving evidence from ancient Egypt. Whatever the hyperbole of the media, some of the archaeological discoveries have genuinely represented significant turning points in the history of the subject, as in the case of the excavation of Aegean-style frescos at the site of Tell el-Dab'a in 1987 or the unearthing of a rich cache of clay tablets inscribed in cuneiform script, at Amarna (the so-called Amarna Letters), in the 1890s. Like the Narmer Palette, both of these finds were quickly recognized not merely as crucial new pieces in the Egyptological jigsaw but as new types of

Treasures of Tutankhamun – Latest

𓈖𓏏𓆑𓄿𓊪𓆑𓏃𓅓𓂋𓇋𓎡𓏏𓂝𓏤𓈖

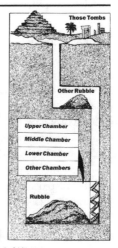

Those Tombs

Other Rubble

Upper Chamber

Middle Chamber

Lower Chamber

Other Chambers

Rubble

TOMB AFTER TOMB OF AMAZING DISCOVERIES REVEALED!

DUST-encrusted archaeologists today abseiled gingerly down through the foetid air of an ancient spiral staircase into the ancient subterranean necropolis of Ben-Gazzara.

There for the first time since 1922 they shone sand-choked torches into what is believed by experts to be Tutankhamun's ancient Department of Trade and Industry, or possibly ancient DVLC.

FABULOUS WEALTH

Rumours quickly spread that there was absolutely no sign of any ancient solid gold sarcophagus or similar.

But as near-exhausted Egyptologists worked in shifts through the hot and stuffy night, a painstaking inch-by-inch search for ancient jewel-encrusted artifacts also drew a disappointing blank.

DRIPPING WITH GOLD

Then suddenly, in the rubble-strewn ancient burial chambers and mud-baked network of ancient tunnels which may once have linked The Boy King's DTI with his once-glorious ancient Office of Fair Trading in Luxor, one or two faded hieroglyphs turned up.

In hushed tones which belied almost hysterical excitement, sweating archaeologists suggested that these almost definitely would fill massive historical gaps in our knowledge of where to find unlooted ancient treasure houses dripping with gold.

INCREDIBLE

Nearby, in the ancient Valley of the Fools, just yards from where the team could easily have stumbled across pile after pile of ancient ceremonial chokers inlaid with rubies, excitement was at fever pitch.

Incredibly, they had unearthed evidence of what once might have been the ancient Mayan DHSS centre at Cairo NE99 2LU.

TREASURES FROM THE TOMB

According to Egyptologist Mortimer van Dijk, mile after mile of ancient labyrinthine corridors, which criss-cross the stygian gloom deep beneath the hot swirling sands, could one day yield an unprecedented ancient horde of rich fragments and/or Aladdin's Cave of fascinating shards.

UNBELIEVABLE

Meanwhile, an ancient piece of papyrus reed, over an inch long and more than likely crafted about 1361 BC into the shape of a vulture's knee, was carefully dusted off.

It stood as unbelievably mute witness to what perhaps were once the ancient workings of The Necropolitan Water Board or North Nile Gas.

Both probably worshipped richly painted vultures, or at any rate finely chiselled she-goats, and surely must have stashed their fabulous takings somewhere round here.

YET MORE MAY BE FOUND

Tomorrow archaeologists will clear ancient debris from an ancient archway, believed once to have soared above an ancient door.

No one knows for certain whether it will indeed prove to be the fabled Lost Door To Tutankhamun's Once All-Powerful VAT Sorting Centre.

A fragment of ancient dust, shown actual size –

Another tell-tale ancient shard is unearthed.

6. Satirical reporting of the discovery of the tomb of Maya.

information, necessitating significant rearrangement of the existing pattern of pieces.

The Tell el-Dab'a frescos

The Austrian archaeologist, Manfred Bietak has been excavating since the 1960s at Tell el-Dab'a, the site of the city of Avaris, capital of the Hyksos rulers from Syria–Palestine, who gained control of northern Egypt during the so-called Second Intermediate Period. The deep stratigraphy at Tell el-Dab'a allows the changing settlement patterns of a large Bronze Age community to be observed over a period of many generations. In the early 1990s the main focus of excavation was the substructure of a large palace building of the early 18th Dynasty at Ezbet Helmi on the western edge of the site. In 1987 many fragments of Minoan wall-paintings were discovered among debris covering the ancient gardens adjoining the palace. Several of these derived from compositions evidently depicting 'bull-leapers', like those in the famous Middle Bronze Age palace at Knossos. Whereas the Minoan and Mycenaean pottery vessels previously found at many New Kingdom sites in Egypt are usually interpreted as evidence of trade with the Aegean, the presence of Minoan wall-paintings at Tell el-Dab'a suggested that the population of Avaris in the early 18th Dynasty (c.1550 BC) may actually have included Aegean families. It has been suggested that the frequent use of a red painted background may even mean that the Tell el-Dab'a Minoan paintings predate those of Crete and Thera (Santorini).

The existence of Minoan wall-paintings, and therefore presumably Minoan artists, at a site within Egypt itself may help to explain the appearance in early 18th-Dynasty Egyptian tomb paintings of such Aegean motifs as the 'flying gallop' (i.e. the depiction of animals' fore- and hindlegs outstretched in full flight). Similar fragments of Minoan paintings have been found at two sites in the Levant (Kabri and Alalakh), where they also appear to be associated with the ruling elite, as at Avaris. This discovery is one of a small number of crucial lynchpins that are potentially able to link together the chronologies of various cultures across the East Mediterranean region.

The find also raises the question of what we mean by 'Minoan' culture. Until the discovery of the Tell el-Dabʿa frescos, it was assumed that Crete was the source of this kind of 'Minoan' art, and that when it appeared elsewhere it was a sign of Cretan contact with other cultures in the Mediterranean, either through trade or population movement. The presence of 'Minoan' art in the Egyptian Delta before it had appeared on Crete suggests that it might have actually originated outside Crete, although the fact that this is so far the only recorded instance of this kind of art in Egypt probably makes it unlikely that Egyptian culture itself was the source.

The Amarna Letters

Like the Tell el-Dabʿa frescos, the Amarna Letters were an unexpected discovery, since they were essentially an 'un-Egyptian' find from an Egyptian archaeological context. They are also similar in their far-reaching implications, since the Amarna Letters have come to exert a significant influence on our understanding of the politics and history of Egypt and the Near East in the late Bronze Age. The story of the Amarna Letters began in 1887 when a number of small clay tablets inscribed with the cuneiform script of Mesopotamia and the Levant were discovered by a village woman digging ancient mud brick for use as fertilizer (*sebakh* in Arabic). This discovery led to further illicit diggings and the appearance of a number of clay tablets on the antiquities market. Their importance was not immediately recognized, and many passed into private hands, but Wallis Budge of the British Museum believed the tablets to be genuine and purchased a number of them. It was Archibald Sayce, Professor of Assyriology at Oxford University at that time, who summed up their significance: 'A single archaeological discovery has upset mountains of learned discussion, of ingenious theory and sceptical demonstration'.

The subsequent excavations of Flinders Petrie at Amarna in 1891–2 revealed a few more tablets, thus confirming that the findspot of the bulk of the tablets was in the centre of the ancient city of Akhetaten, almost certainly from beneath the floor of a building identified by stamped mud bricks as 'Place of the Letters of Pharaoh', as well as nearby structures. A few more tablets were found by German and British excavators at Amarna in the first few decades of the 20th century, bringing the total to 382, spread between the collections of the British Museum, the Bodemuseum in Berlin, the Louvre, and the Egyptian Museum in Cairo, but most of the finds came from the initial illicit digging rather than scientific excavations, making their precise origins uncertain. Their exact chronology is also still debated, but they span a 15–30-year period, beginning around year 30 of Amenhotep III (1391–1353) and extending no later than the first year of Tutankhamun's reign (1333–1323), with the majority dating to the reign of Akhenaten (1353–1335). Most are inscribed with texts in a dialect of the Akkadian language, which was the lingua franca of the time, although the languages of the Assyrians, Hittites, and Hurrians (Mitanni) are also represented.

The majority of the documents in the archive are items of diplomatic correspondence between Egypt and either the great powers in Western Asia, such as Babylonia and Assyria, or the vassal states of Syria and Palestine. They provide a fascinating picture of the relationships between Egypt and these states, although there are very few letters from the Egyptian rulers, the vast majority being the letters sent *to* them by other rulers. One interpretation of the letters is that they document the disintegration of the Egyptian Empire during the reign of Akhenaten, the so-called 'heretic pharaoh', who left few records of military campaigns and is therefore assumed to have neglected foreign policy in favour of a programme of religious and political reforms within Egypt itself. An alternative view would be that we happen by chance to have these documents from Akhenaten's reign, and that similar archives from earlier or later in the New Kingdom, had they survived, might contain equally desperate pleas for assistance from Syro-Palestinian cities under siege. In other words, it might be argued that our view of Egyptian influence over Syria–Palestine is largely based on the Egyptians' own accounts of their battles and victories, and that the chaotic state of affairs documented in the Amarna Letters might have actually been the normal condition of the Egyptian 'Empire' throughout the New Kingdom rather than being a temporary aberration.

Another controversy that has emerged out of the translation and interpretation of the Amarna Letters is the question of who the 'Apiru are. Many of the tablets from Syro-Palestinian vassals refer to a group of people called the 'Apiru, who appear to have been widespread across the Near East throughout the 2nd millennium BC. Since the first translations of the letters spelt the name Hapiru or Habiru, biblical scholars immediately began to explore the possibility that these were the first references to Hebrews, some even specifically correlating references to 'Apiru attacks with the account of Joshua's invasion of Canaan. However, there has not yet been any conclusive proof that the ethnic terms 'Apiru and Ibri (Hebrew) are linked etymologically, and it is not even clear whether 'Apiru refers to an ethnic group, a social group, or an economic class (or all three), with one commentator suggesting that the term was synonymous with 'social banditry'. As John Laughlin points out, in *Archaeology and the Bible*, 'it is certainly true to say that not all 'Apiru were Hebrews. Whether any Hebrews were ever 'Apiru is, at the moment, an open question.'

As well as giving insights into the political conditions of the time, the letters also shed light on trade relations and the values of particular commodities such as glass, gold, and the newly introduced iron, while the various forms of address employed in the letters indicate the standing of the writers *vis-à-vis* the Egyptian court. A very enterprising conference held in 1996 (and published in 2000, as *Amarna Diplomacy*, eds. Cohen and Westbrook) brought together historians, social scientists, and professional diplomats to discuss such topics as 'international law in the Amarna age', 'diplomatic signalling', and a 'socio-psychological' analysis of Amarna diplomacy. This innovative combination of expertise takes the study of the letters into areas not previously contemplated by Egyptologists.

Apart from being subjected to new textual analysis, the Amarna tablets have also begun to be studied from a more scientific point of view. Dr Yuval Goren, an Israeli geology lecturer, has used petrographic analysis to study the actual clay from which they were formed. The aim of his work is to compare the clays with the geology of various sites in the Mediterranean, the Near East, and North Africa in order to try to work out the places from which the letters were sent. Using this method, Goren tackled the question of the whereabouts of the kingdom of Alashiya, which was associated with the supply of copper to Egypt and other countries, and which might have been located in Cyprus, Cilicia, north-west Syria, or even southern Israel. The fabric of one of eight Alashiya letters in the British Museum looked quite different, suggesting that, unlike most of the tablets, it might not be an Egyptian-made local copy but might possibly be one of the original letters made from clay at Alashiya itself. It was made from a pinkish marly clay that includes many fragments of chlorite and dolerite, suggesting that the clay was obtained from a particular type of area dominated by igneous rock. Goren found that this helped to narrow down the likely choices to the Troodos massif on Cyprus, the region of Kizzuwatna in Anatolia and the Biabashin region of north-west Syria. He was then able to rule out first Kizzuwatna, because it was governed by Egypt's great rivals, the Hittites, and secondly the north-west Syrian area, because it seemed to be too geologically diverse to fit the bill. On Cyprus, on the other hand, there was one region that fitted the evidence in various ways. Geologically, the likely area was located between the doleritic Troodos mountains and the adjacent marly part of the island, which would have provided a pink clay with a mixture of dolerite and marly clay just like that of the tablet. Significantly, this area of Cyprus is also the area in which copper was being produced from the Middle Bronze

Age onwards. Cyprus itself had always been the favourite candidate for the location of Alashiya, but Goren's analysis seems to provide good scientific support for the theory.

Although most of the Amarna archive consists of letters, it also includes 32 other kinds of texts that do not seem to have been directly connected with international diplomacy. These tablets were probably related to scribal education and the process of translation itself, including a dictionary-like list of Akkadian and Egyptian words, a fragment of a syllabary, as well as several scribal exercises and literary texts. We therefore not only have the royal correspondence itself, but also some of the evidence for the activities of the scribes employed to write and translate the letters.

Wilbour's Phoenician rolls, Petrie's New Race, and other embarrassments

Our steadily adjusted and reframed picture of Egyptian civilization has periodically allowed earlier finds to be reviewed and reinterpreted, sometimes quite radically. Although the circumstances of the discovery of the Tell el-Dab'a frescos and the Amarna Letters were quite different (and separated in date by around a century), both were nevertheless fairly rapidly recognized as important finds. There are, however, many instances of important finds that were at first totally misinterpreted or regarded as unremarkable, and only came to be recognized as really significant sources of evidence long after the discovery had been made. For instance, the American Egyptologist Charles Wilbour bought nine sealed papyrus rolls from local women at Elephantine between 1890 and 1893. He assumed at first that they were inscribed in some kind of Phoenician script, and, although he eventually deduced that the script was actually Aramaic (spoken and written throughout the Near East in the 1st millennium BC), he simply put them into storage and they were not published until 1953, after his daughter had bequeathed them to the Brooklyn Museum. In fact these documents – along with others that emerged in later excavations on Elephantine – turned out to be among the most important written sources for life in Egypt during the First Persian Period.

Surprisingly, a good example of a great discovery that was initially completely misunderstood comes from the career of the great Flinders Petrie. In his excavation of the Naqada cemeteries in 1895 he found that virtually all of the graves comprised rectangular, sometimes brick-lined, pits containing one or more bodies in foetal positions, placed on reed mats with the head oriented towards the west. Occasionally the bodies appeared to have been deliberately dismembered before burial, and there were some indications of human sacrifice. The varying quantities of grave goods usually consisted of some combination of pottery, stone vessels, slate palettes, flint knives, beads, bracelets, and figurines. Petrie immediately recognized that these were quite different to conventional Egyptian burials, but his conclusion that they belonged to a 'New Race' from outside Egypt, who had supposedly invaded Egypt at the end of the Old Kingdom, was to turn out to be drastically wrong, both chronologically and ethnically. The most galling aspect of getting this wrong from Petrie's point of view was the fact that one of his great rivals, Jacques de Morgan, came up with the correct solution when he published a similar set of graves at Abydos. The people buried in the Naqada and Abydos cemeteries were different not because they were a 'new race' but because they were the Egyptians of late prehistory whose long sequence of culture preceded the pharaonic period, and had until then been virtually unknown. As if to make amends for his colossal error, Petrie went on to use the Naqada material to develop the ingenious 'sequence dating' system. This typological system enabled him to create the first Predynastic chronology, which many would rate among his greatest achievements.

Conversely, some of the most famous finds made in Egypt have not necessarily had very significant effects on our views of Egypt. Howard Carter's discovery of the tomb of Tutankhamun, for instance, obviously had enormous impact on the public awareness of Egyptology from the 1920s onwards, but, apart from providing the first tantalizing glimpse of the sumptuous range of equipment which must once have been contained in the tombs of much more renowned and long-lived pharaohs, such as Amenhotep III and Ramesses the Great, it included very little genuinely new historical data. Arguably Carter's greatest achievement was to raise the public profile of Egyptian archaeology to a much higher level, but the contents of the tomb did not take the subject in any new directions or change opinions on any great historical debates (apart from the possibility that the calcified blood clot at the base of Tutankhamun's skull might show that he was murdered). The tomb is of course arguably the most exciting find in the history of archaeology, and its contents have increasingly yielded information on various aspects of the technology of the 14th century BC – but Egyptologists can be very difficult to please . . .

7. 21st-century fieldwork in Egypt, geophysical survey at Saqqara.

Egyptology embracing science

As a result of the increasing application of innovative methods of survey, excavation, and analysis, the professional Egyptologist has begun to require at least a nodding acquaintance with a number of scientific disciplines, such as bioanthropology, geology, genetics, and physics. This process of expansion has added strength to the subject , with each of these different academic disciplines providing fresh sources of stimulation and new directions for future research.

In Carter's time, science was only just beginning to have an effect on the world of Egyptology, primarily in the form of a man called Alfred Lucas, who, within four years of the discovery of Tutankhamun's tomb, was to publish the first edition of *Ancient Egyptian Materials and Industries*, a brilliant summary of the surviving evidence for Egyptian materials and craftwork, which served as the essential manual for Egyptological science until the 1990s. Lucas was a chemist working in Cairo, who had access to much of the material in the Egyptian museum, enabling him to publish data, chemical analyses, and bibliographical references for a great deal of the most important material excavated since the mid-19th century, including the objects from the tomb of Tutankhamun.

When the British Egyptologist Eric Peet gave his inaugural lecture as Reader in Egyptology at Oxford University in 1934, he chose to discuss 'the present position of Egyptological studies'. Already acutely conscious of the impact of science on Egyptology, he suggested that

> many of the questions, especially those of the origins of materials and the technical processes of the arts and crafts, which have puzzled us for years, will eventually reach definite solution through the resources of chemistry and the other sciences.

Certainly there are two aspects of Egyptology that have been repeatedly affected by science over the 70-year period since Peet's lecture: first, the use of science has meant that some elements of the archaeological record that were previously regarded as relatively uninformative, such as soil and seeds, have begun to produce as much information as more traditional finds, such as sculptures and papyri. Second, the application of scientific techniques has allowed more information to be squeezed out of conventional types of evidence. Mummified bodies, instead of simply being unwrapped and examined externally, can now be x-rayed in various ways, without even removing the wrappings, and DNA samples can reveal a great deal more about the nature and identity of the specific human or animal concerned. Inorganic objects, such as stone vessels, can also be analysed more extensively now. Stone artefacts can be studied not only in terms of their shape, size and decoration but also with regard to the type of rock from which they were made: where it came from, how it was extracted, and what techniques were used to transform it into a prestige funerary item.

An important area of progress in recent years has been the use of geophysical methods of prospecting prehistoric and pharaonic sites, including the application of such techniques as resistivity survey, proton-magnetometer survey, sonic profiling, ground penetrating radar, and thermal imaging. In the Great Pyramid at Giza, for instance, the combined use of microgravimetry (a technique for measuring the relative densities of stone blocks) and the transmission of electromagnetic microwaves revealed the possible presence of hidden chambers behind the stone walls of the so-called 'king's' and 'queen's' burial chambers. On a less sensational level, resistivity surveys at Saqqara, Memphis, and el-Amarna, during the 1980s and 1990s, have proved particularly suited to Egyptian sites. Resistivity traverses and magnetometry have supplemented conventional survey techniques, allowing archaeologists both to select areas showing the greatest potential for excavation and to map major features, such as wells or enclosure-walls, without having to remove the material under which they are buried. For example, Edgar Pusch, the director of excavations at Qantir (the site of the ancient city of Piramesse), has been able to use caesium magnetometry to publish detailed 'street-plans' of brick-built urban areas that are still unexcavated.

Another growth area in the late 20th and early 21st century has been the study of human diet in pharaonic Egypt, based principally on the analysis of surviving fragments of food both from domestic and funerary contexts. Recent projects of this type have included studies of Egyptian bread and beer making, wine production, and meat processing. Many other aspects of Egyptian technology have begun to be explored, with the use of innovative scientific approaches to the archaeological remains of the pharaonic period, including experimental and ethno-archaeological work.

Applying science to the Narmer Palette

The Narmer Palette was carved from a type of rock technically known as siltstone, which was used for large funerary and votive palettes in the Predynastic period. By the Early Dynastic period this versatile material was even being used for sculpture, including the statue of the 2nd-Dynasty ruler Khasekhemwy, which was found near the Narmer Palette at Hierakonpolis, and is now in the Egyptian Museum, Cairo.

The hard green siltstone, greywacke, and conglomerate used by the ancient Egyptians belong to the Hammamat Series of late Precambrian age and are widely distributed in the northern and central parts of the Eastern Desert. This stone, in common with many other types of stone used by the ancient Egyptians, has been frequently misidentified by Egyptologists over the years. It has often been described as 'slate', although in fact the pronounced foliation (layering) and conspicuous flaking and splitting that characterize slate are absent from the Hammamat siltstone. The so-called 'slate' palettes of the Predynastic period are actually of siltstone, and the rock is identical to that used for stone vessels and statuary in the pharaonic period. 'Schist' is another name that has previously been applied wrongly to the dark green Hammamat rocks. Schist is a metamorphic rock with large mineral grains in distinct layers, completely unlike the fine-grained, homogeneous siltstone of Wadi Hammamat. Dark grey to black siltstone and greywacke are occasionally confused with basalt, a crystalline, igneous rock formed directly from lava. Ironically, the English word 'basalt' actually derives from the ancient Egyptian word for siltstone – *bekhen* – via the Greek word *basan* and the Latin *basanites*.

Where did the 'Narmer Palette stone' come from? In fact, only one ancient Egyptian quarry for this type of stone is known, although others must presumably have existed. The quarry, located in the Wadi Hammamat, was worked from the Predynastic through to the Roman Period (*c.*4000 BC–AD 500). Over 250 inscriptions and numerous quarry workings occur along a stretch of the wadi just over a kilometre in length, west of the confluence with Wadi Atolla. A Roman ramp runs up the south side of the wadi, while on the floor of the wadi on the north side are the ruins of a chapel of the 30th Dynasty. The green conglomerate workings are at the west end of the quarry, where there are numerous quarried blocks left by the Romans. The Romans had a very descriptive name for the stone quarried at Wadi Hammamat: *lapis hecatontalithos* ('stone of a hundred stones'). Italian stonemasons, who recycled stone brought to Italy by the Romans, called the Hammamat siltstone *breccia verde antico* or *breccia verde d'Egitto*, and this is the origin of the frequently encountered name 'green breccia'. However, in modern terminology, breccia is a rock composed of angular fragments, whereas in conglomerates such as siltstone the fragments are rounded.

The ways in which the siltstone has frequently been confused and misidentified highlight the problems faced by Egyptologists in identifying and correctly naming the various categories of stone from which Egyptian artefacts and buildings were made. In defence of the Egyptologist, it should be remembered that modern scholars are already required to master a variety of skills within the ever-expanding subjects of Egyptian archaeology and philology, and can therefore hardly be expected to acquire sophisticated geological training overnight. And this is the nub of the problem: many of the geological errors and misconceptions in the Egyptological study of stone artefacts result purely from archaeologists' and museum curators' lack of access to geological knowledge.

If it were simply a question of all Egyptologists agreeing to describe Egyptian alabaster as travertine or black granite as diorite or gabbro, then the transformation would be relatively easy, although experience shows that even widely accepted changes in terminology can take a long time to permeate the literature. However, what would be required would be the geological re-evaluation of most of the stone sculptures and artefacts currently in museums or excavation storerooms, to say nothing of the attempt to rewrite countless excavation reports where the excavator has used idiosyncratic personal systems of geological categorization (e.g. Petrie's use of the term marble to refer to coloured limestones).

A striking contrast can usefully be drawn with the study of Egyptian pottery, which, during the last two decades of the 20th century, moved inexorably – and beneficially – from the age of subjective description to a more rigorous era of thin-sectioning and objective analysis, including the application of the so-called 'Vienna system' of fabric description as well as the use of statistical sampling and other methods of quantification. If the study of ceramics can be so radically changed, why does the identification and analysis of stone-types lag so far behind? One crucial difference between the two is that ceramics have increasingly become the preserve of certain Egyptologists who have chosen to specialize in ceramology, whereas the need to identify stone arises in a number of different areas of study, from the technological analysis of functional objects, such as quern-stones or door-sockets, to the aesthetic appraisal of royal statuary and early prestige goods such as palettes and mace-heads. There is no reason why a similar subdiscipline of geological Egyptologists should not emerge, but in practice the knowledge of stone-types would need to spread through the subject much more extensively than has tended to be the case with pottery.

Chapter 3

History: building chronologies and writing histories

One of the fundamental questions often asked about the Narmer Palette is whether, as its discoverers assumed, it was created as a record of a specific historical event: the military triumph on which the first unified kingdom of Upper and Lower Egypt was founded. The palette and various other 'protodynastic' artefacts have long been regarded as lying at the interface of prehistory and history in ancient Egypt. The term protodynastic was invented to describe the crucial period encompassing the late Predynastic and the beginning of the Early Dynastic period. The 'Predynastic' was the last few hundred years of the long prehistoric period in the Nile Valley, while 'Early Dynastic' refers to the first few centuries of the dynastic or pharaonic period (see timeline at the back of the book).

At the time of the discovery of the Narmer Palette, the Predynastic period was barely known at all, since it was not until the following year that Flinders Petrie would publish the first chronological framework for late prehistory, using 'sequence dates' based on changing fashions of artefacts in grave goods at the Predynastic Naqada cemeteries. This means that the chronological context of the palette would have been seen quite differently by Quibell and Green compared with modern researchers. Whereas most Egyptologists now see this crucial artefact as part of the culmination of a long sequence of late Predynastic cultural development, including a developing corpus of decorated palettes, its discoverers regarded it as the first real 'document' in recorded history, emerging almost magically out of what seemed then to be the darkness of prehistory. The palette immediately began to be interpreted as a record of the first truly significant historical 'event' in Egyptian history: the military defeat of Lower Egypt (the Delta region in the north) by the ruler of an expanding Upper Egyptian kingdom.

When the British Egyptologist Bryan Emery made the first real attempt to summarize the nature of Early Dynastic Egypt with the publication of his *Archaic Egypt* in 1961, a great deal of the primary evidence was freshly excavated, much of it by himself and his contemporaries or immediate predecessors. There was also, of course, a large quantity of evidence that had not yet been excavated, particularly with regard to the thousands of years preceding the emergence of the early Egyptian state. When Emery was writing, Egyptian prehistory, like many other aspects of the modern discipline, was still very much in its infancy, so it is not surprising to find that he constantly looks forwards into the pharaonic period for comparisons and analogies that can anchor his subject as a specific stage of the Egyptians' cultural development. In contrast, recent books and articles on Early Dynastic Egypt tend to be more firmly rooted in the late Predynastic. Indeed the German excavators who have been re-examining the early cemeteries at Abydos have increased the evidence for the existence of a politically and/or culturally united Egypt well before the 1st Dynasty by their work in the late Predynastic area near the royal cemetery (so-called Cemetery U), where they have found probable 'royal' tombs that are earlier than the time of Narmer, thus demonstrating that certain elements of

Egyptian kingship (including a late Predynastic model royal sceptre, carved from ivory) stretched back at least 150 years earlier than the beginning of the 1st Dynasty.

Many modern Egyptologists have used explicitly anthropological approaches to the study of the formation of the state in early complex societies, but for Emery's generation of archaeologists, the 'culture history' approach was still the main paradigm in archaeology. As the Canadian archaeologist Bruce Trigger puts it,

> Almost all cultural change in the archaeological record was attributed to the diffusion of ideas from one group to another or to migrations that had led to the replacement of one people and their culture by another . . . The latter fashion is exemplified in the work of W.M.F. Petrie, who, in discussing the prehistoric development of Egypt, explained all cultural changes in terms of mass migrations or the arrival of smaller groups who brought about cultural change by mingling culturally and biologically with the existing population. Petrie saw no possibility of significant cultural change without accompanying biological change.

Bryan Emery was keen to promote the idea that the emergence of Egyptian civilization at the end of the 4th millennium was the result of the invasion or immigration of the so-called Dynastic Race (or 'Followers of Horus') from Mesopotamia. Now, however, the massive advances in our knowledge of prehistory and recent excavations of Predynastic and early Dynastic sites, particularly the early royal necropolis at Abydos and the city and cemetery at Hierakonpolis, have demonstrated extremely convincingly that the development and inauguration of the pharaonic age was largely an indigenous Egyptian phenomenon, arising steadily, and almost inevitably, out of processes of late Predynastic social, economic, and political change within the Nile Valley. A recent history of early Egypt (Toby Wilkinson's *Early Dynastic Egypt*) makes this very point: 'The various trends which led to the formation of the

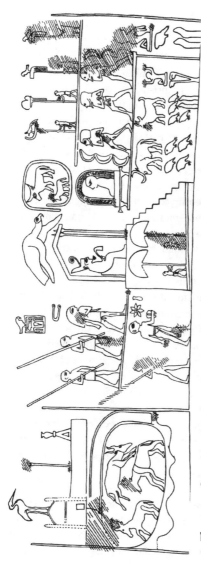

8. The scenes decorating the 'Narmer mace-head', c.3000 BC.

Egyptian state were gradual processes which began in the early Predynastic period.'

Palettes, mace-heads, and history-writing

The Narmer Palette is just one of a number of surviving elite artefacts primarily comprising votive palettes, mace-heads, and ivories from late prehistory and the first two dynasties. These items of so-called 'mobiliary art' (i.e. art that can be carried around) provide a rich corpus of early Egyptian iconography and early hieroglyphs, and, as we will see in the chapter on writing, the distinction between pure symbols and words is a difficult one to make at this date. Single items, or groups of objects, have often been used to create theories concerning the emergence and unification of the early pharaonic state. Several other significant palettes and mace-heads were also found by Quibell and Green at Hierakonpolis, including fragments of a large limestone ritual pear-shaped mace-head that also bears the signs spelling out the name Narmer. This appears to show not war-like scenes but ones that are more obviously to do with early rituals associated with kingship, one of which is interpreted as the first known version of the ritual known as *ḫ'ty-bity*: 'the appearance of the King of Lower Egypt'. Just as the Narmer Palette has been interpreted by many Egyptologists as a literal narrative account of the defeat of Lower Egypt by Narmer, ruler of Upper Egypt, so the mace-head was once widely regarded as a memorial of Narmer's marriage to a 'northern princess'. This theory relied primarily on the assumption that a depiction of a beardless figure in a carrying-chair was a representation of the royal bride, but it has been pointed out that the seated figure might be the image of a deity, and not even necessarily a female one.

In addition to the Narmer mace-head, fragments were found of another limestone mace-head of a similar type (now in the Ashmolean Museum, Oxford), this time decorated with raised relief scenes, including a man wearing the Upper Egyptian White

Crown. This individual is the largest figure on the mace-head, and appears to be identified by the ideogram hovering in front of him as King Scorpion, who might have been Narmer's predecessor on the throne. The figure of Scorpion is grasping a large hoe, while a servant holds out to him a basket, perhaps in order to catch the earth that he is removing from the ground. The fact that he and his servant are standing immediately beside some kind of water-course has led to suggestions that he is ritually excavating an irrigation canal with the help of attendants. As a result of this interpretation, which is widely held but not necessarily conclusively proven, the Scorpion mace-head has frequently been used as a crucial piece of evidence in the hypothesis that the Egyptian state, and its characteristic monarchical style of government, emerged through the control of water by an elite group.

The Canadian Egyptologist Nick Millet argues that the purpose of the images and texts on the palettes and mace-heads of the late 4th and early 3rd millennia was not to describe historical events in themselves but simply to label, commemorate, and date. He suggests, quite convincingly, that the artefacts' decoration was intended to communicate the contemporary 'context' of the object in terms of event and ritual. He demonstrates this specifically through his analysis of the Narmer mace-head, which he claims to be a depiction of royal rituals enacted in a single year, probably the one in which the mace was created and brought as a votive gift to the temple. Millet suggests that the scenes on the mace-head resemble the brief lists of rituals given for each year of the kings' reigns on the Palermo Stone (see the section on building chronologies, later in this chapter, for a discussion of this early Egyptian 'king-list').

Our analysis of the scenes and texts on objects such as the Narmer Palette and mace-head is generally complicated by our modern urge to be able to distinguish between 'real' events and rituals. But the ancient Egyptians show very little inclination to distinguish consistently between the two, and indeed it might be argued that Egyptian ideology during the pharaonic period – particularly in so far as it related to the kingship – was reliant on the maintenance of some degree of confusion between real happenings and purely ritual or magical acts. The texts and artefacts that form the basis of Egyptian history usually convey information which is either general (mythological or ritualistic) or particular (historical), and usually our aim in constructing Egyptian historical narrative is to distinguish as clearly as possible between these types of information, taking into account the ancient Egyptians' tendency to blur the boundaries between the two.

With regard to the palettes and mace-heads, Donald Redford suggests that there must have been a need to commemorate the unique events of the unification at the end of the 3rd millennium BC, but that these events were 'commemorated' rather than 'narrated'. This distinction is a crucial one: we cannot expect to disentangle 'historical' events from scenes that are commemorative rather than descriptive, or at least if we do so we may often be misled.

This debate concerning rituals, symbols, and historical events was given an intriguing new twist by one of the discoveries made by the German excavation team re-examining the royal burials at Abydos. In 2000, while sifting through one of the many spoil heaps left behind both by the ancient conversion of the tombs into shrines (see Chapter 7) and by 19th- and 20th-century excavators, they found an almost complete ivory label which appears to be decorated with images that closely resemble some of those on the Narmer Palette. Like most other surviving examples of this kind of label found both in the Early Dynastic royal tombs and the late Predynastic elite burials of Cemetery U, it was made in order to identify the quality, quantity, and year of delivery of a product (usually a vessel containing imported oil) placed in the tomb. A small hole bored in the top right-hand corner was intended to attach it to the vessel, and the lower of two lines of incised hieroglyphic inscription identified it as '300 units of first-quality oil'.

It is the upper line of inscription on the Narmer label that is the most relevant to our discussion, however, since it closely resembles the smiting scene on the Narmer Palette, except that in this instance the image is transformed into a form of hieroglyphic sentence comprising the name Narmer, which appears twice, once on the right-hand side in a *serekh* frame (as on the palette) and once in the middle of the inscription but this time with two arms having been added to the *nar* hieroglyph (the catfish sign) so that it can wield a mace in one hand and grasp a bearded foreigner in the other. The foreigner sprouts papyrus plants from his head (like the schematic man held prisoner by the Horus falcon on the palette) and has a small 'bowl' hieroglyph to his left. At the top left a vulture hovers over a rectangle perhaps representing the royal palace, with a falcon-topped standard in front of it. This is very plausibly interpreted as the sentence 'Smiting the Libyan marshland people by Horus Narmer, celebration (of victory) of the palace'. Since it presumably identifies a specific year in the king's reign, as the other labels do, it seems likely that it identifies the same year as the scenes depicted on the Narmer Palette. In addition, a tiny ivory cylinder bearing the name of Narmer was found at Hierakonpolis and probably also belongs to the same year in his reign, since it shows the catfish smiting three rows of foreign captives identified with the same word *tjehenw* (usually translated as Libyans). Taken together, the label, the cylinder, and the palette seem to confirm Millet's idea that the labels and the votive items are all decorated with information describing a particular year in a king's reign. The excavator of the label, German Egyptologist Günter Dreyer, argues that this combination of evidence proves that Narmer's defeat of northerners/Libyans was an actual historical event. This assessment, however, seems rather premature. An alternative assumption would be that we simply now have three records of the same event, but we are no closer to knowing whether it was (*a*) a genuine historical military victory, (*b*) purely a kingship ritual with no basis in reality, or (*c*) a ceremonial re-enactment of some actual earlier triumph.

What is Egyptian history?

In defining Egyptian history scholars are inevitably attempting to impose upon the Egyptian sources modern concepts and categories that would often have had no real meaning or relevance to the ancient writers. The types of ancient Egyptian texts that are usually described as 'historical' invariably had a very different function when they were originally composed; they therefore have to be carefully interpreted if genuinely historical data are to be extracted from them.

In the *Cambridge Ancient History*, William Hayes argues that there are only three surviving Egyptian historical texts that would conform to a definition such as that given by Redford; these are the inscriptions of Kamose (two hieroglyphic texts on stelae and the hieratic Carnarvon Tablet, *c*.1555–1550), describing this late 17th-Dynasty ruler's battles against the Hyksos, the annals of Thutmose III (1479–1425) describing his campaigns in Syria–Palestine, and the stele of Piye (750–712) describing his conquest of Egypt. Redford adds to these Hatshepsut's speech inscribed in the Speos Artemidos rock-temple, a possibly fictional speech made by Ramesses III (1194–1163) at the end of the Great Harris Papyrus, and Osorkon's description of the Theban rebellions in the Third Intermediate Period (1070–712). A further text which may now be added to this list is a fragment of the annals of Amenemhat II (1929–1892) discovered at Memphis in the mid-1950s but not published until 1980, which shows that something closely approximating to the modern concept of history was already being compiled in the Middle Kingdom (2040–1640), in the form of detailed records of the political and religious events from each year of a king's reign.

Notwithstanding the few exceptions listed above, the vast majority of such narrative-structured and ceremonial texts surviving from Egypt were concerned much more with preserving and transmitting national traditions or with fulfilling a particular religious or funerary role, rather than being attempts to present objective accounts of the past. The Swiss Egyptologist, Erik Hornung describes the ancient Egyptians' view of their past as a kind of 'celebration' of both continuity and change.

Even the supposedly historical fragments of Egyptian texts, such as the Kamose stelae and the Annals of Thutmose III (1479–1425), are effectively components of the temples in which they were found, therefore they differ considerably from the true historical tradition inaugurated by the Greek historian Herodotus in that they incorporate a high degree of symbolism and pure ritual. The contents of the monumental texts and reliefs on the walls of Egyptian tombs and temples are often much more related to the symbolic and static world of myth than to history. There is a common tendency to regard myth as a form of 'primitive history', but this is rarely the case. Redford makes a good distinction between myth and history:

> Their meaning [i.e. the meaning of myths] has nothing to do with their having occurred in the past, but rather with their present significance ... Horus's championing of his father, the upliftings of Shu, the murder of Osiris – these are all primordial events, timeless and ever-present; and neither king nor priest who re-enacts them can be said to fulfil an historic role, or to be commemorating 'history'.

Building chronologies

History is nothing but a shapeless mass unless it is structured according to some kind of chronological basis, and there are numerous ways in which Egyptologists have set about creating such a framework for ancient Egypt, using a complex mixture of archaeological data (such as coffins bearing different types of decoration), texts (such as 'king-lists' and stelae), and scientific dating methods (such as radiocarbon dating and thermoluminescence).

The term 'king-list' is used by Egyptologists to refer to a number of ancient Egyptian lists of the names and titles of rulers, some of which also incorporate information concerning the length and principal events of individual reigns. Virtually all of the surviving examples derive from religious or funerary contexts and usually relate to the celebration of the cult of royal ancestors, whereby each king established his own legitimacy and place in the succession by making regular offerings to a list of the names of his predecessors. The king-lists have survived in various forms, mostly dating to the New Kingdom, but the earliest is the so-called Palermo Stone, a large fragment of a basalt stele in the Palermo Archaeological Museum, Sicily, which dates to the 5th Dynasty (c.2494–2345).

The Palermo Stone is inscribed on both sides with hieroglyphic texts describing the reigns of the kings of the first five dynasties, as well as the preceding era of mythological rulers. The original stele is estimated to have been about 2.1 m long and 0.6 m wide, and four smaller fragments of it have survived (now in the Egyptian Museum, Cairo, and the Petrie Museum, University College London). We have no information about its original findspot, since the main fragment appeared on the antiquities market in 1866, but without provenance. The text comprises the annals of the kings of Lower Egypt. It begins with many thousands of years taken up by mythological rulers up to the time of Horus who is then said to have given the throne to Menes. His successors are listed up to the 5th

Dynasty. The text is divided into a series of horizontal registers divided up by vertical lines, incurved at the top, to represent the hieroglyph for regnal year (*renpet*). Into each compartment was written memorable events for that year and the height of the inundation. The events recorded were mostly religious festivals, wars, and the creation of particular statues. The name of the ruler concerned is written above the relevant block of compartments. It is frustrating to know that a record detailing every ruler up until the end of Dynasty 5, along with the lengths of their reigns, once existed but that only fragments of it are within our grasp.

Another tantalizing surviving fragment is the 'Mitrahina day-book', which is a reused Old Kingdom relief block inscribed with the earliest known example of Middle Kingdom royal annals. This section of annals from the reign of the 12th-Dynasty pharaoh Amenemhat II was itself later reused in the New Kingdom temple of Ptah, near the modern village of Mitrahina, which occupies part of the site of the ancient capital city of Memphis. Unlike the Palermo Stone, which simply summarizes events (many of them probably rituals) for each year of the various kings' reigns, the Mitrahina inscription provides quite detailed information for parts of two years of Amenemhat II's reign.

The Turin Papyrus (also known as the Turin Royal Canon) was a simple list of rulers compiled in the reign of the 19th-Dynasty ruler Ramesses II (1290–1224), giving the precise duration of each reign, and occasionally a summary of the number of years that had elapsed since the time of Menes, whom the Egyptians seem to have regarded as the first ruler of the pharaonic period. This hieratic papyrus, now in the Museo Egizio, Turin, was removed from Egypt by Bernardino Drovetti. It was then almost complete, but it suffered badly before entering the Turin collection and, like other king-lists, is now incomplete. The work of such mid-19th-century Egyptologists as Jean Francois Champollion and Gustavus Seyffarth led to the numerous fragments being placed in the correct order, although many lacunae still remain. Originally it must have contained around 300 names, even including the Asiatic 'Hyksos' rulers of the Second Intermediate Period (although with a sign to indicate that they were foreigners, and no royal cartouche shape around the names), and ending with Ramesses II. Like the Palermo Stone, the list attempted to go back beyond the reigns of known kings and to assign reign lengths to the unnamed spirits and gods who had supposedly ruled before the coming of the first pharaoh. The severe damage done to this extremely significant document is another great tragedy.

The five principal monumental king-lists also date to the early 19th Dynasty: these are the two Abydos King-lists (found in the Abydos temples of Seti I and Ramesses II respectively, the latter now in the British Museum), the Karnak King-list (now in the Louvre), the Saqqara Tablet, which derives from the tomb of Thuneroy, a high official of Ramesses II (now in the Egyptian Museum, Cairo), and a scene in the tomb of the priest Amenmes at Thebes (TT373, c.1300 BC), showing him venerating the statues of 13 previous rulers. There are also a few much briefer king-lists, such as a graffito at the mining and quarrying site of Wadi Hammamat, dated palaeographically to the 12th Dynasty (1991–1783), which consists of the names of five 4th-Dynasty rulers and princes. A seal impression discovered by German archaeologists at Umm el-Qa'ab in 1985 is one of the shortest surviving king-lists, but it shows just how useful texts of this kind can be. It lists six rulers in the following order: Narmer, Aha, Djer, Djet, Den, and Merneith, thus providing another crucial piece of evidence that the king depicted on the Narmer Palette was probably the earliest in the sequence of 1st-Dynasty rulers.

Finally, the most detailed historical source is the *Aegyptiaca*, a history of Egyptian rulers compiled by a Hellenicized Egyptian priest called Manetho in early Ptolemaic times (3rd century BC), which has unfortunately survived only in the form of extracts quoted by much later historians from Josephus (1st century AD) to

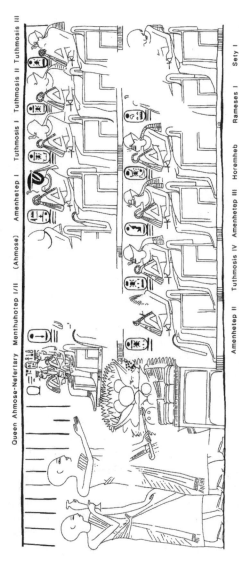

9. The 'king-list' from the tomb of the priest Amenmes at Thebes, c.1300 BC.

George Syncellus (early 9th century AD). Manetho was evidently able to consult both Egyptian sources, such as the king-lists described above, and also Greek annals. He probably wrote his history (dedicated to Ptolemy II) during the time that he was employed at the temple of Sebennytos, near the modern town of Samannud in the Delta. His division of the sequence of earthly (i.e. post-mythological) rulers into 30 dynasties (to which a 31st, the 2nd Persian Period, was later added) has been a major influence on the conventional view of Egyptian chronology since the early 19th century.

However, as the sources of Egyptian historical and archaeological data have inexorably expanded and diversified, with translations of new texts and excavations of fresh sites, it has become apparent that Manetho's chronological system is fatally flawed through its basic assumption that there was one long sequence of Egyptian rulers governing over the entire country, without overlaps between reigns and without fragmentation into mini-kingdoms. Over the years, research has increasingly demonstrated that Egypt was, at various times, not culturally unified and politically centralized, with changes taking place at different speeds in the various regions. Other analyses show that short-term political events, which have tended to be regarded as the paramount factors in history, may often have been less historically significant than the gradual socio-economic processes that can change the cultural landscape more overwhelmingly in the long term.

There are in fact several major problems with traditional chronology. First, Manetho's history is frequently unreliable because we only have surviving quoted fragments rather than the whole original text, and because we do not know his sources. Second, there is often uncertainty regarding the lengths of kings' reigns: for instance, the Turin Canon says that Senusret II and III have reigns of 19 and 39 years, whereas their highest recorded regnal years on monuments are 6 and 19. Third, there has been a major problem with the so-called 'intermediate periods', which have been traditionally somewhat lazily interpreted as 'dark ages'. Fourth, there is still considerable controversy concerning overlaps between succeeding reigns (known as coregencies), especially in the 6th and 18th Dynasties. Finally, much of the chronology hinges on ancient astronomical observations (particularly of the 'heliacal rising' of the dog-star Sirius), which can provide different absolute dates depending on where the ancient astronomer-priests made their observations. Some Egyptologists, such as Rolf Krauss, have suggested that all the sightings were made at one place (e.g. Elephantine), but others, such as William Ward, have argued that they must have all been local observations, i.e. the religious festivals timed to coincide with astronomical events might actually have taken place on different days in different parts of the country. One document from Lahun dates a heliacal rising of Sirius to the seventh year of the reign of Senusret III, which would convert into an 'absolute' date of 1872 BC if the observation was made in Elephantine, and 1830 BC if it was made in Heliopolis – a difference of considerably more than the average ancient Egyptian's life-span (which in the 19th century BC is estimated to have been around 35 years even for elite men and 30 for elite women, the latter dying earlier on average because of the perils of ancient childbirth).

The significance of the most basic historical divisions (i.e. the distinctions between the Predynastic, pharaonic, Ptolemaic, and Roman periods) has begun to be questioned. On the one hand, the results of excavations during the 1980s and 1990s in the cemeteries of Umm el-Qa'ab at Abydos suggest that before the 1st Dynasty there was also a Dynasty 0 stretching back for some unknown period into the 4th millennium. This means that, at the very least, the last one or two centuries of the 'Predynastic' were probably in many respects politically and socially 'Dynastic'.

Conversely, the increasing realization that late Predynastic pottery types were still widely used in the Early Dynastic period shows that certain cultural aspects of the Predynastic period continued on into the pharaonic period. The long 'pre-Dynastic' periods of Egyptian prehistory are inevitably understood as sequences of cultural rather than political developments. Now the Dynastic period (as well as the Ptolemaic and Roman periods) has begun to be understood with regard not only to the traditional sequence of individual kings and ruling families but also to the types of fabric being used for pottery, and the styles and materials of many other types of artefact.

Whereas there are definite political breaks between the pharaonic and Ptolemaic periods, and between the Ptolemaic and Roman periods, the gradually increasing archaeological data from the two latter periods has begun to create a situation where the process of cultural change may be seen to be less sudden than the purely political records suggest. Thus it is apparent that there are aspects of the ideology and material culture of the Ptolemaic period that remain virtually unaltered by political upheavals. Instead of the arrival of Alexander the Great and his general Ptolemy representing a great watershed in Egyptian history, it might well be argued that, although there were certainly a number of significant *political* changes between the mid-1st millennium BC and the mid-1st millennium AD, these took place amid comparatively leisurely processes of social and economic change. Significant elements of the pharaonic civilization may have survived relatively intact for several millennia, only undergoing a full combination of *cultural and political* transformation at the beginning of the Islamic period in AD 641.

The preceding discussion introduced the nuts and bolts of chronology-building in Egypt, but to understand how they work in practice we need to look at a suitable case-study.

The Qasr el-Sagha temple: a case-study in dating things

At the site of Qasr el-Sagha, on a low hill by the desert cliffs at the north-eastern corner of the Faiyum, 50 miles (75 km) south-west of

10. The unfinished temple at Qasr el-Sagha.

Cairo, is a large stone building which was obviously some kind of religious monument. Unlike many other surviving religious buildings, however, this one was left undecorated, uninscribed, and incomplete. The lack of inscriptions means that we know neither who built it nor what divine cult was celebrated there. The question therefore arises: how do Egyptologists go about dating a large anonymous stone structure like this?

The temple is built from blocks of dark brown calciferous sandstone. The scientific technique of 'optically stimulated luminescence' (OSL), which can measure the amount of time since a stone block was last exposed to sunlight, could in theory provide a date for the construction of the masonry, but no one has yet attempted this at Qasr el-Sagha. Another, more traditional, possibility is to date the building's architectural style. It measures 33 x 16 feet (10 x 5 m) in total area, and consists of seven shrines and a long offering room. We can probably assume that if the temple had been completed it would have had a court or pillared hall (or both) in front of it. It was during the Middle Kingdom that the generally mud-brick local cult temples began to be rebuilt in stone, and there are two 12th-Dynasty temples that are comparable with the one at Qasr el-Sagha, although both have been much modified by 18th-Dynasty and Ptolemaic phases of reconstruction. The first is a tripartite shrine at Medamud, 5 km north of Thebes, which was dedicated to the local god Monthu and built by the 12th-Dynasty ruler Senusret III on top of an earlier mud-brick complex. The second is the sandstone temple of Renenutet (a cobra-form harvest-goddess) at Medinet Maadi (Narmouthis) in the south-western Faiyum region. It was founded during the reigns of Amenemhat III and IV (1844–1787) at the end of the 12th Dynasty, but, like the Medamud shrine, was later expanded and embellished during the Greco-Roman period. The inner part of the temple consists of a small papyrus-columned hall leading to a sanctuary comprising three chapels, each originally containing statues of deities. The likelihood is that the Qasr el-Sagha temple was also dedicated to a group of local gods, whose statues would have been placed in the seven shrines. This suggests that the rough date is 12th-Dynasty, and as for the specific king concerned, Dieter and Dorothea Arnold, who studied the temple in the 1970s, decided that Senusret II was perhaps the best candidate, since he left more than his fair share of unfinished temples (probably due to the relative brevity of his reign), although on the same basis Amenemhat IV would also be a possibility.

Architectural style is a relatively tenuous dating criterion, so the conscientious archaeologist would tend to look for further confirmation by some other means. In the case of Qasr el-Sagha, potential dating evidence exists nearby in the form of a rectangular, planned settlement measuring about 374 x 260 feet (115 by 80 m), with an adjacent cemetery. To the north-east of the main settlement is a slightly larger but more amorphous area of mud-brick housing. Both settlements have been partially excavated and dated to the 12th Dynasty by the pottery found there. Like the roughly contemporary Middle Kingdom pyramid-town of Kahun, the rectangular village apparently housed a specialized 12th-Dynasty community under direct state control.

There is a further twist to the dating problem of the Qasr el-Sagha temple. The site as a whole appears to be linked by an ancient paved road with the basalt quarries of Gebel Qatrani quarries, about 6 miles (10 km) to the north. The obvious assumption might be that the settlements and temple relate directly to the quarries' exploitation, but it has been pointed out by a number of scholars that basalt was mainly used in the Old Kingdom and Late Period and indeed that the small amount of pottery associated with the quarry road itself is primarily Old Kingdom in date. We are therefore left with a temple and two settlements of the 12th Dynasty, which is one of the very periods when the site's likely raison d'être, basalt quarrying, seems to have been in decline.

Possibly the origins of Qasr el-Sagha might have been as a very small quarry-workers' settlement (although there are as yet no traces of Old Kingdom activity at the site), which by the Middle Kingdom had developed into a different kind of community with some as yet unknown function perhaps connected with the empty, unfinished temple. This goes to show that dating something is a long way from understanding it. Barry Kemp cautions against excessive concentration on dating in Egyptology, if it distracts us from understanding the phenomena in question:

> Chronology enables us to follow changing patterns over time and to chart progress towards our own modern world. But too great a concern with 'history' – with dates and the chronicling of events – can become a barrier to seeing the societies and civilizations of the past for what they really were: solutions to the problems of individual and collective existence which we can add to the range of solutions apparent in the contemporary world.

Historical change and material culture

As the dating of the Qasr el-Sagha settlements indicates, one of the most effective dating methods used by the modern Egyptologist is the study of the styles and fabrics of pottery vessels. There has been an enormous growth in the study of Egyptian pottery in the last 20 years, both with regard to the quantity of sherds being analysed (from a wide variety of types of site) and in terms of the range of scientific techniques now being used to extract more information from ceramics. Inevitably the improvement in our understanding of this prolific aspect of Egyptian material culture has had an impact on the chronological framework. The excavation of part of the city of Memphis (the site of Kom Rabi'a) in the 1980s provides a good instance of the ways in which more sophisticated approaches to pottery have enabled the overall process of cultural change to be better understood.

Pottery vessels can be arranged in sequences of relative date by such traditional techniques as seriation of cemetery material and the analysis of large quantities of stratified material at domestic or religious sites, but they can also be given fairly precise absolute dates either by the conventional method of association with inscriptions or datable visual images (particularly in tombs) or by the use of such scientific techniques as thermoluminescence dating. Some scholars have begun to study the ways in which vessel and fabric types change over the course of time. Thus, the form of pottery bread moulds, for instance, underwent a dramatic change at the end of the Old Kingdom, but it is not yet clear whether the source of this change lies in the social, economic, or technological spheres of life, or whether it is merely the result of a change in 'fashion'. Such analyses show that processes of change in material culture took place for a whole variety of reasons, only some of which were linked to the political changes that tend to dominate conventional views of Egyptian history. This is not to deny the many connections between political and cultural change, such as the correlation between centralized production of pottery in the Old Kingdom and resurgence of local pottery types during the more politically fragmented First Intermediate Period, and then the renewed homogenization of pottery during the more unified 12th Dynasty.

In the study of certain phases of Egyptian history, such as the emergence of the unified state at the beginning of the pharaonic period or the decline and demise of the Old Kingdom, scholars have sometimes examined environmental and cultural factors in order to explain sudden important political changes. One of the problems with this *selective* attention to non-political historical trends, however, is the fact that we still know so little about environmental and cultural change during periods of stability and prosperity, such as the Old and Middle Kingdoms, that it is much more difficult to interpret these factors at times of political crisis. The increased study of pottery vessels and other common artefacts (as well as environmental factors such as climate and agriculture) are beginning to create the basis for more holistic versions of Egyptian history, in which political narratives are viewed within the context of long-term processes of cultural change.

The application of seriation to private coffins of the Middle Kingdom has produced very useful chronological and historical data. The traditional classification of Middle Kingdom coffins, introduced by Mace and Winlock, had distinguished only two basic types: (1) the northern style (from the Memphite region, Beni Hasan, el-Bersha, and Meir), and (2) the southern style (from Asyut, Akhmim, Thebes, Gebelein, and el-Moalla). The main difference between the two types was supposed to be the fact that most of the decoration was confined to the exterior in the southern type, and also that human figures were not portrayed on the northern examples. Thus, for instance, the sarcophagi of Mentuhotep II's wives, from Thebes, were decorated with scenes of hairdressing, similar versions of which can be found on coffins from Gebelein and el-Moalla. Some 'southern' coffins also included so-called 'star clocks' on the underside of the lids, and lines of text invoking the astronomically linked deities Nut, Sopdet (Sirius), Sah (Orion), and Ursa Major.

In the 1980s, this traditional typology was thoroughly revised by Harco Willems. He argued that there were several basic elements in the decoration of Middle Kingdom coffins: eyes, false door, objects frieze, offering formula, invocations of deities, Coffin Texts, Book of Two Ways, Star clocks, and that these indicated a number of flaws in Mace and Winlock's typology. First, there were no grounds for the southern and northern division, and each regional type was distinctive in its own right – thus Asyut coffins could be demonstrated to be quite different from el-Bersha examples. Secondly, there was an overall typological change over time within the decoration of the so-called 'Herakleopolitan' type (which he prefers to call 'standard') that could be used to date coffins and therefore also to date the archaeological contexts from which they derived.

The new Willems typology would not in itself have been of such significance, if it had not been for the fact that coffins were such a common type of find from such a large number of Egyptian sites that they represented an enormous source of chronological potential that could now be properly tapped. Willems's 'seriation' of the coffins not only allowed the objects themselves to be more effectively dated, but also meant that groups of coffins could be used to establish links between the changing local and national political leaders, thus allowing local and national transformation to be correlated. The way ahead in construction of Egyptian chronologies must surely lie in this kind of research, since king-lists and the like can only tell us about limited aspects of political change (the rise and fall of dynasties and individual rulers), whereas chronological frameworks based on particular elements of Egyptian material culture from sites throughout the country can provide information on the history of ancient Egyptian society and economy.

The need for Egyptologists to free themselves from a largely Manetho-style view of Egyptian history (in which the past is regarded as an elaborated king-list) is eloquently expressed by the German Egyptologist Stephan Seidlmayer in his preface to an account of the First Intermediate Period:

Much of Egyptian history tends to concentrate on the royal residence, the kings, and 'court culture', but in writing the history of the First Intermediate Period it is necessary to focus instead on provincial towns and on the people themselves, who make up the most basic elements of society.

This statement should be applied to the writing of Egyptian history in general.

Chapter 4

Writing: the origins and implications of hieroglyphs

Egyptian hieroglyphs consist of ideograms (signs employed as direct representations of phenomena such as 'sky' or 'man') as well as phonetic signs representing the sound of all or part of a spoken word, therefore the connections between writing and art were much stronger in pharaonic Egypt than in many other cultures. In the hieroglyphic script decorating buildings and sculptures, the writing of simple words such as 'goose' or 'head' was to some extent an artistic exercise as well as an act of verbal communication. A third type of hieroglyph is the 'determinative', which is so-called because it 'determines' the meaning of the entire word. Thus, for example, a variety of words meaning food, drink, or the process of eating conclude with a determinative comprising a man holding his hand up to his mouth, and more abstract words, such as 'to know' or 'to hear', are followed by a determinative in the form of a rolled up papyrus, indicating that these words are concerned with thought and intellect.

Many of the surviving texts from ancient Egypt were created in order to complement and annotate the paintings and reliefs decorating the surfaces of the walls and ceilings of temples and tombs. Both the appearance and function of Egyptian writing and art were therefore closely connected with religious beliefs and funerary practices, and the Egyptians were firmly convinced of the real physical potency of words and images. Indeed, in many inscriptions on tomb-walls or funerary equipment, it was considered necessary to remove certain portions of hieroglyphs, such as the legs of bird-signs, in order to incapacitate forces that might prove malevolent to the deceased. This sense of the magical potential of verbal and artistic representations was expressed in the funerary ritual known as the 'opening of the mouth', with which both the mummies and statues of the deceased were thought to be imbued with new life – a variant of this ritual seems to have been performed each morning in Ptolemaic temples in order to bring to life the texts and images on the walls.

The Narmer Palette and the origins of Egyptian writing

Like many early artefacts, the Narmer Palette includes symbols that have been interpreted either as purely pictorial elements, as strings of unconnected pictograms, or even as organized, grammatical sentences. What does this tell us about current views concerning the origins and nature of writing in Egypt?

The pictorial narrative on the palette appears to be complemented by hieroglyphs such as the 'catfish' and 'chisel' signs that hover in front of the smiting figure of the king. These two signs have the phonetic values *nar* and *mer* respectively in pharaonic times, but it is not clear whether they are used here phonetically or ideogrammatically. The *nar-mer* signs are repeated at the top of each side of the palette, framed in a *serekh*, which is a powerful symbol of kingship, probably representing the entrance to an early royal palace. We know that this *serekh* symbol was used from the late Predynastic period onwards as a way of framing and indicating one of the king's names (known to Egyptologists as his 'Horus name' because the *serekh* often has a Horus falcon perched protectively over it). There are, however, also a number of other signs on this side of the palette, which most Egyptologists interpret as early hieroglyphs (see description in Chapter 1 above). Opinions differ as to whether the four symbols at the top right of this side of the palette (immediately above the ten decapitated bodies) are hieroglyphs or pictures.

In 1961, Alan Gardiner went so far as to describe the palette as a 'complex of pictures which the spectator would then translate into words'. He does not seem to have meant this literally, but simply as a way of describing the interpretive process of deciphering the iconography. In 1991, however, an American Egyptologist, Walter Fairservis, junr, published an article arguing that previous Egyptologists' interpretations of the Narmer Palette had been subject to 'a significant methodological flaw' because they had treated most of the decorated surface of the palette as pictorial rather than linguistic. Fairservis took the view that all of the symbols on both sides of the palette should be translated into grammatical phrases, written in an early version of the Egyptian hieroglyphic system. In other words he argued that, instead of interpreting the palette as a combination of art and writing, it should be literally *read* as one long sentence. He identified 62 putative 'hieroglyphs', and discussed the possible nuances of meaning contained in each of them, then assembled them into a form of text, on the basis of which he claimed that the palette was 'not documentation of the unification of Upper and Lower Egypt, but instead represents a victory by the leader of the Edfu district over the Nile valley south into Nubia'. This theory is not generally accepted by other Egyptologists, but it does raise the question of the extent to which late Predynastic and Early Dynastic art includes fully developed writing of the spoken language, as opposed to conveying information through purely artistic images.

Recent studies on the origins of the Egyptian writing system have focused on several specific questions. When did the hieroglyphic system first begin to be used, and when did it begin to incorporate phonetics and grammar? Was it adopted from another culture (the most likely candidate being the Near East, where writing seems to have emerged in Mesopotamia at a slightly earlier date), or did it emerge independently in Egypt, and if so could it have been 'invented' by a single individual or a small group of innovators, as opposed to evolving slowly over a number of generations or centuries?

Another question that tends to be asked about all early writing systems is whether they emerged through practical bureaucratic requirements or whether their initial development was much more concerned with ritualistic and ceremonial purposes. Were the earliest Egyptian hieroglyphs a kind of propagandist tool used by rulers and elite groups to preserve their own power? The answer to this question is complicated by the fact that our views of the dates at which writing emerged in different cultures, and also the purposes for which it was initially used, are very much determined by the kinds of materials used as writing media (e.g. clay tablets, bone labels, rolls of papyrus, and stone monuments), and by their ability to survive in the environmental conditions that prevail in different parts of the world. Because the clay tablets used for administrative records in early Mesopotamia were well preserved by the local conditions, they gave the impression, to some scholars, that writing had emerged to serve bureaucratic purposes, whereas in Mesoamerica, China, and Egypt, it appeared that the earliest inscribed objects (such as Maya stone stelae and Egyptian stone palettes) were used for ceremonial purposes, primarily concerned with the maintenance of power by an elite group. This cross-cultural view of writing, in which the original purposes of writing in Mesopotamia are contrasted with those evidently prevailing in other areas, ignores the fact that, by their very nature, administrative archives in most early societies will tend to have been inscribed on cheaper, less durable materials (such as papyrus in Egypt, which is known to have been in use as early as the 1st Dynasty). These low-cost bureaucratic materials will therefore not tend to survive very well, whereas the earliest ceremonial and 'propagandist' texts are characteristically written on highly durable materials (primarily stone), which are therefore more likely to have survived. Of course it might also be argued that the idea of making a binary distinction between administrative and ceremonial/propagandist texts is a slightly dubious one, given that some of the early texts from Egypt (such as the bone and ivory labels attached to items in the rich late Predynastic/Dynasty 0 tombs) might be defined as elaborate elite-style versions of relatively prosaic bureaucratic documents.

Can we date the beginning of Egyptian writing?

Turning to the date at which writing emerged in different parts of the world, and the mechanisms by which it was developed or adopted, the general assumption, until comparatively recently, was that the first examples of the Sumerian cuneiform writing system appeared significantly earlier than the Egyptian hieroglyphs. It was therefore further assumed that the first Egyptian texts, which seemed to have emerged relatively abruptly at the end of the 4th millennium BC, were probably inspired by increased Egyptian links with the Near East. However, since the actual signs making up the two systems (Sumerian cuneiform and Old Egyptian hieroglyphs) were so different, few scholars believed that the Egyptian system had evolved directly out of cuneiform, and it tended to be suggested by some Egyptologists that it might have been the basic *idea* of pictographic writing that came from Mesopotamia.

These assumptions have been somewhat unravelled by archaeological discoveries made by German archaeologists at Abydos during the 1990s, suggesting not only that the hieroglyphic script might have already begun to be used in the middle of the Predynastic period (perhaps *c*.3500 BC), but also that the use of

11. Labels from tomb U-j at Abydos, showing early hieroglyphs, c.3200 BC.

phonetic signs might have appeared much earlier than previously thought. The excavations at tomb U-j, the impressive burial of a ruler called Scorpion (evidently an earlier Scorpion than the owner of the mace-head found near the Narmer Palette) revealed one room containing numerous small labels carved from wood and bone that appear to bear clearly recognizable hieroglyphs consisting of numbers, commodities, and possibly also place-names or royal agricultural estates. The importance of these hieroglyphic labels is that they are almost certainly not just pictorial signs ('ideograms'), which would represent a much more basic stage in the history of the script. Instead, many of them are representations of sounds in the spoken language ('phonograms'), a stage in the development of the script that was not thought to have occurred until at least the 1st Dynasty. The German philologists who studied the labels were able to identify them as phonetic symbols because they often spelt out the names of well-known towns frequently mentioned in later inscriptions, such as Buto and Bubastis.

It therefore appears that the bureaucrats employed by the earliest rulers at Abydos – at least 200 years before the 1st Dynasty – were already using a sophisticated form of Egyptian script involving phonetic signs as well as ideograms. The fact that this writing often seems to refer to Lower Egyptian place-names as the sources of goods placed in an Upper Egyptian ruler's tomb is also very strong evidence that the northern and southern halves of Egypt were already closely connected economically – and perhaps politically too. Thus many of the factors associated with fully developed states – such as writing, bureaucracy, monumental architecture, and complex systems of exchange and economic control – were evidently in place in Egypt at a time when the culture is still conventionally regarded as 'prehistoric'.

Use and abuse of texts in Egyptology

The beginning of Egyptology as a complete historical discipline, comprising the study of both texts and archaeology, was made possible by Champollion's decipherment of Egyptian hieroglyphs in 1822. By the late 1820s, the demotic script had also been deciphered (largely by Thomas Young) – thus, within a single decade, Egyptology had been transformed from prehistory into history. By the 1860s, Charles Goodwin and François Chabas had deciphered and translated many papyri inscribed with the hieratic script, thus ensuring that texts in all four Egyptian scripts (hieroglyphics, hieratic, demotic, and Coptic) could now be understood.

The translation of a whole range of documents, containing such information as the names of gods and kings, as well as the details of religious rituals and economic transactions, soon enabled the field of Egyptology to take its place alongside the study of the classical civilizations. Champollion's discovery, however, had also set in motion an inexorable process of academic divergence between linguists and excavators, between textual studies and the investigation of material culture.

Almost from the moment that hieroglyphs, hieratic, and demotic began to be translated, Egyptology was increasingly characterized by a struggle to reconcile the kinds of general socio-economic evidence preserved in the archaeological record with the more specific historical information contained in ancient texts. While the newly discovered knowledge of the texts had the potential to revive the very thoughts and emotions of the ancient Egyptians, it also introduced a temptation to assume that the answers to questions about Egyptian civilization could be found in the written word rather than the archaeologist's trench. The purely archaeological view of Egyptian culture, as it was preserved in the form of buried walls, artefacts, and organic remains, would henceforth always have to be seen in the context of a richly detailed corpus of texts written on stone and papyrus. The absence of written records in prehistoric archaeology may be frustrating, but it has undoubtedly allowed prehistorians greater freedom to evolve new theories and hypotheses that are based purely on the surviving material culture. In Egyptian archaeology, as in other historical disciplines, the written word, with all its potential for subjectivity and persuasion, has a paradoxical tendency to obscure – and sometimes even eclipse – the archaeological evidence.

It is interesting, from the point of view of the dichotomy between texts and archaeology, to compare the history of Egyptian archaeology with that of modern Maya studies. Mayanists appear to have experienced the reverse situation: their discipline was predominantly anthropological and archaeological until Maya glyphs began to be deciphered in the 1980s, producing a sudden flood of texts in the Mayan language, which have significantly altered the perception of the Maya culture. The suspicion with which Maya archaeologists initially regarded the historical information provided by their philological colleagues presents a mirror-image of the reaction of many traditional text-based Egyptologists to the increasingly science-based and anthropological analyses of pharaonic Egypt produced by archaeologists in recent years. Both Mayanists and Egyptologists are struggling to come to terms with the basic fact that writing tends to be the product of elite members of society whereas the bulk of archaeological data derives from the illiterate majority of the population; the solution lies in the successful integration of these types of evidence to produce a view of society as a whole.

According to the French theoretical archaeologist Jean-Claude Gardin,

> it is taken for granted that archaeology can deal with all the paraphernalia of ancient man without limitations. Yet, some restrictions are still common, if only implicit. One of them is a result of the current opposition between … inscribed materials and ancient texts on the one hand, to be studied by epigraphists and historians, and material objects on the other hand, left to the competence of archaeologists or prehistorians.

There have, in the past, been many syntheses of ancient Egyptian textual and archaeological material, but increasingly, as the sheer amount of both types of data continues to grow, Egyptological studies tend to be split between linguists and archaeologists in the way that Gardin describes. Barry Kemp's discussion of the administration of Nubia in the Middle Kingdom, employing both textual and archaeological data, indicates that textual sources can usually only reveal fragments of systems, whereas archaeology can suggest the 'broad structural outlines in society'. Textual evidence, on the other hand, can often supply the individual details that help to transform abstract socio-economic processes into something that is closer to conventional history. In 1974, David O'Connor put forward a relatively optimistic view of the combined use of archaeological and textual data in Egypt, arguing that

> the two data-sets are essentially complementary; the archaeological record contains historical information only faintly reflected in the textual, and vice versa. The interpretation of each is frequently corrected and amplified by reference to the other.

Chapter 5
Kingship: stereotyping and the 'oriental despot'

Both of the faces of the Narmer Palette are decorated with war-like scenes of the king, but it is the large depiction of the king smiting a foreigner with his mace on the reverse of the palette that is probably the most potent image. The royal smiting scene is one of the commonest images in Egyptian art, serving as a metaphor for the power of the pharaoh, who preserves the order of the universe by ritually subduing the forces of chaos. In 1899, the year after the discovery of the Narmer Palette itself, a Predynastic version of the smiting scene was found by Frederick Green at Hierakonpolis, on the wall of Tomb 100, which was built for a local ruler at around 3300 BC, and is the first surviving Egyptian tomb to contain painted decoration. Almost a century later, in the 1990s, an even earlier example of the motif, showing a tall figure smiting three crouching captives, was found painted on a pottery vessel excavated from the Predynastic tomb U-239 at Abydos (dated to the late Naqada I period, *c*.3500 BC). This classic icon of the smiting pharaoh was to

12. **Faience chalice from Tuna el-Gebel, *c.*925 BC, showing several images of the king smiting captives.**

retain its significance for thousands of years, appearing in a variety of religious and artistic contexts, from amulets and stelae to the walls and pylons of temples as late as the Roman period.

13. Gneiss statue of king Khafra from Giza, 4th Dynasty, *c.*2500 BC.

One theme that repeatedly appears in Egyptological studies is
the nature of the Egyptian king, and particularly his relationship
both with his fellow mortals and with the Egyptian pantheon.
The Narmer Palette already establishes a close link between the
king and the falcon-god Horus, with its depiction of the divine
falcon holding a foreign captive in front of Narmer. The
interaction between king and god in the act of conquest conveys

some of the complexity of the symbolism and metaphors surrounding the ancient Egyptian conceptions of kingship. The idea of the despotic pharaoh has found its way into the modern consciousness via many different means, from the Bible to Shelley, and Egyptologists have frequently used the debate concerning Egyptian kingship to explore such topics as the changing nature of the Egyptian political system, and the question of what we can know of the identities of the various pharaohs as real individuals (as opposed to iconographical ciphers). In the case of Egyptian rulers, so many of their mummified bodies have survived (especially from the New Kingdom) that we are in the unusual position of being able actually to gaze into their faces as if they were our contemporaries, while simultaneously examining the long-ruined monuments and surviving texts from their reigns.

For the Egyptians, the reign of each new king represented a new beginning, not merely philosophically but practically, given the fact that dates were expressed in 'regnal years'. This means that there would probably have been a psychological tendency to regard each new reign as a fresh point of origin. Every king was essentially reworking the same universal myths of kingship within the events of his own time. By the Old Kingdom, the kings each held five names (the so-called 'fivefold titulary'), each of which encapsulated a particular aspect of the kingship: three of them stressed his role as a god, while the other two emphasized the supposed division of Egypt into two unified lands.

Many rulers held the titles 'mighty bull' and 'bull of Horus' (and note that both of the depictions of Narmer on the palette show him wearing a bull's tail hanging from his waist as part of the royal regalia). The figure of the bull trampling a fallen foreigner and breaking through the walls of a city, depicted on the lower part of the front of the Narmer Palette, is probably symbolic of the king's victory over foreign territories. This strong identification between

14. Granite sphinx of Amenemhat III from Tanis, 12th Dynasty, c.1820 BC.

king and bull continued throughout the pharaonic period. There was perhaps an element of punning involved in the king/bull correlation, in that the Egyptian term for bull was *ka*, which was phonetically identical to another word often used to refer to the king's divine counterpart or 'double'.

In any king's names and iconography a great deal of metaphor and symbolism was involved, making it difficult for modern scholars to use these kinds of evidence to arrive at a sense of the particular characteristics and activities of individual kings, as opposed to the general idea of kingship. In reading Egyptologists' accounts of the reigns of various pharaohs, we have to take into account two kinds of stereotyping and pigeonholing: first, the stereotypes that the original Egyptian texts present us with and, second, the unconscious stereotyping of which Egyptologists themselves are often guilty.

Amenhotep the athlete

One particular 'victim' of regal stereotyping was Amenhotep II, who is repeatedly portrayed on his monuments as a great sporting hero. Thus, Alan Gardiner, in 1961, described him as follows:

> His muscular strength was extraordinary: we are told that he can shoot at a metal target of one palm's thickness and pierce it in such a way that his arrow would stick out on the other side; unhappily the like had been related of Tuthmosis III, though with less detail, so that we are not without excuse for scepticism. Nonetheless there are other examples of his athletic prowess too individual to be rejected out of hand.

In the 1980s, the French Egyptologist Nicolas Grimal even saw these traits in Amenhotep's names and epithets:

> [He] is remembered as a far less intellectual ruler ... His main claim to fame was his unusual physical strength ... This taste for

strength is apparent in Amenophis' titulary: his Horus name was 'powerful bull with great strength' or 'with sharp horns' and his Golden Horus name was 'he who siezes all the lands by strength' . . . Amenophis tested his strength in three Syrian campaigns.

The problem of whether Amenhotep II was an unusually athletic king, however, is much more a question of unpicking stereotypical details from idiosyncratic facts.

First, is it simply a case of accident of survival, whereby more texts concerning athleticism happen to have been preserved from the time of Amenhotep II than from other reigns? Second, if it is not an accident of survival, do we interpret this as an indication that the king was actually a great sportsman or do we simply credit him with making an enormous contribution to the *idea* of the Egyptian king being a great athlete?

The American Egyptologist Peter Der Manuelian believes that Amenhotep II was actually both a genuine sporting enthusiast and a vigorous promoter of this aspect of the kingship:

> it is fair to cite Amenophis as the most vigorous advocate of athletic endeavours, and he certainly expanded the parameters of this particular literary genre with some truly original and very detailed passages, especially in the cases of rowing, horsemanship and archery. These unparalleled passages lend credence to a relatively accurate description of this aspect of his character. Yet there remains the separate question of truth versus exaggeration in the athletic texts. Could Amenophis actually pierce copper targets, and successfully wield an oar twenty cubits in length? . . . But if we choose to remain dubious of the veracity of Amenophis' texts, this royal exaggeration on the part of the king does little to change our conclusions here. Indeed the archaeological record corroborates the textual evidence. Amenophis' tomb in the Valley of the Kings (no.35) produced a composite bow of wood and horn.

Hatshepsut: female pharaoh or proto-feminist?

When confronted by the question of individual pharaohs' distinctive personalities, as preserved in the visual and textual record, many Egyptologists, and a number of other scholars, have naturally been tempted to speculate as to their characters and motivations. This second question in particular leads on to discussion of two specific rulers whose reputations have stretched beyond Egyptology: Hatshepsut (the female pharaoh) and Ramesses the Great. These individuals have been the object of much-debated attempts to characterize them psychologically, and often enough to stereotype them.

Hatshepsut is one of a very small group of women (perhaps five altogether) who managed to rule Egypt in their own right, rather than as appendages of male rulers. The term 'queen' is frequently applied to royal females in Egypt but Egyptologists use it at their peril, since there is no real ancient Egyptian word for a female ruler, only a few phrases used to describe women related by blood or marriage to the ruling male (principally the 'great royal wife' (*hemet weret nesw*), the 'royal mother' (*mwt nesw*) and the 'royal wives' (*hemwt nesw*)). This meant that in those rare situations when women became 'kings' themselves they were virtually obliged to adopt male regalia and attributes. Certainly Hatshepsut, who is the female ruler for whom most evidence has survived, had herself portrayed for much of her reign as if she were physically male. In her cult temple at Deir el-Bahari and in other monuments she is frequently shown in male kingly costume, including the royal 'false beard'. There must presumably have been some sense of conflict between her sex and the masculine role of the pharaoh, but only the posthumous erasures of her name from monuments have survived as indications of such feelings of inappropriateness. Interestingly, her royal names and titles are regularly written with feminine grammatical endings (and one of them perhaps deliberately recalls one of the names of the Middle Kingdom female ruler Sobekneferu), producing a set of wordplays connecting her with certain deities and aspects of divinity that would have not been possible within a male king's nomenclature.

Almost certainly because of Hatshepsut's gender, there has been a tendency for many Egyptologists to stereotype her as a pacifist. In 1951, for instance, John Wilson argued that

> The reigns of Hat-shepsut and of Thut-mose III contrast strongly in the activities of the state. She records no military campaigns or conquests; he became the great conqueror and organizer of empire. Her pride was in the internal development of Egypt and in commercial enterprise ... The unusual prominence given to this venture [i.e. the expedition to Punt] has meaning as an expression of policy, that Egypt should cultivate more intensively the friends they already had and let the unfriendly Asiatics suffer from their own stubborn hostility because Egypt would not deal with them.

Ten years later, Alan Gardiner stated this even more baldly: 'The reign of Hatshepsowe had been barren of any military enterprise except an unimportant raid into Nubia', and Nicholas Grimal's history of Egypt, published in the 1980s, argued that her only real foray into the outside world was the trading mission to the land of Punt:

> This expedition [to Punt], recounted in great detail on the walls of Hatshepsut's mortuary temple, represented the high point of a foreign policy that was limited to the exploitation of the Wadi Maghara mines in Sinai and the despatch of one military expedition into Nubia ... During the reign of Hatshepsut the only military actions were to consolidate the achievements of Tuthmosis I ...

In the 1960s, however, the Canadian Egyptologist Donald Redford had already put forward a revisionist view of the queen's reign, suggesting that unjustified assumptions were being made on the basis of an apparent lack of evidence rather than actual facts. He makes the point that some male rulers might be regarded (probably wrongly) as pacifists if the same conclusions were drawn on the basis of a paucity of texts describing military expeditions,

> The military achievements of Hatshsepsut are bound to suffer eclipse through the unfortunate circumstance that her reign was followed by the most brilliant imperial expansion in Egypt's history ... If it is true that Thutmose III's campaigns contrast most strikingly with her efforts in the military sphere, an even greater contrast must appear between the reigns of Thutmose and those, say, of Haremhab and Sheshonk I. Solely on the basis of extant texts we should have to conclude that the reigns of the latter two monarchs were almost devoid of foreign wars.

In the case of Haremhab, we have ample evidence from his pre-royal career as Tutankhamun's general to know that he was anything but a pacifist.

Another debate concerning the reign and personality of Hatshepsut centres on the two closely connected questions of whether she was a weak ruler who used an unusual amount of propaganda to bolster her claims to the throne and whether she was unusually dominated by her (male) steward Senenmut. So we find Gardiner suggesting in 1961 that:

> It is not to be imagined however that even a woman of the most virile character could have attained such a pinnacle of power without masculine support. The Theban necropolis still displays many splendid tombs of her officials, all speaking of her in terms of cringing deference. But among them one man stands out preeminent.

A similar view was taken by Donald Redford in 1967:

> There can be no doubt that her chief supporter was her steward Senenmut, a man of low origin, who throughout most of her reign appears to have been something of a power behind the throne ...

She had a circle of favourites, a motley collection of individuals with no common background and little reason to share political goals ... Some time after year 16 Senenmut disappeared. Whether his fate was a natural death or a fall from favour and assassination, we do not know ... Thutmose III, a man in his prime and a born soldier, quickly filled the vacuum created by the departure of Senenmut and Neferure, and Hatshepsut must have been forced to adopt a conciliatory attitude to him if she wished to salvage anything.

Redford goes on to argue that Hatshepsut was then gradually eclipsed as Thutmose III began to appear more often in reliefs and was delegated the task of undertaking foreign wars – however, none of this was different to any other coregency between a king and his successor: Egyptian princes generally were given greater prominence in order to prepare them for the kingship.

Even in the 1980s, Grimal was still promoting the image of a weak Hatshepsut dominated by Senenmut, the sinister power behind the throne:

During her reign she relied on a certain number of prominent figures of whom the foremost was a man called Senenmut. Even in Senenmut's time there was spiteful gossip suggesting that he owed his good fortune to intimate relations with the queen ... Senenmut was a ubiquitous figure throughout the first three-quarters of Hatshepsut's reign, but he subsequently seems to have fallen into disgrace for reasons which are not precisely known. It is thought that after the death of Neferure ... he may have embarked upon an alliance with Tuthmosis III which led Hatshepsut to discard him in the nineteenth year of her reign, three years before the disappearance of the queen herself.

However, Grimal's references to 'spiteful gossip' and 'disgrace' owe more to his imagination than to any actual sources of evidence.

This time it is a French Egyptologist, Suzanne Ratié, who rides gallantly to Hatshepsut's rescue:

> The personality of Senenmut was therefore rich and complex. Certain aspects of his career are impenetrable. It seems that his influence is visible in all the great achievements of the reign at least until year 16. It is difficult to differentiate the role played by the queen and her 'advisor' in various decisions and activities. We use the term 'advisor' to describe Senenmut, but we deliberately avoid the use of the term 'favourite', for this aspect of the lives of Hatshepsut and Senenmut is completely out of our reach and does not rest on any objective evidence.

Finally, a third historical debate concerning Hatshepsut centres on the way in which she seems to have justified her right to the throne. There are a very small number of royal monuments from the New Kingdom that contain claims that the ruler in question was the result of sexual intercourse between a deity (the god Amun) and a woman, thus suggesting that he (or, in Hatshepsut's case, she) was physically semi-divine. This raises the question as to whether such scenes might perhaps have survived by chance only from certain reigns, but might originally have been standard parts of many royal monuments, or whether – as many Egyptologists have argued – some rulers were more concerned to stress their legitimacy than others.

Egyptologists have frequently speculated as to whether these so-called 'scenes of divine birth' of Hatshepsut and Amenhotep III, at Deir el-Bahri and Luxor temple respectively, were propagandistic or religious documents (or perhaps both at the same time). It has been frequently argued that Hatshepsut's gender forced her to come up with new methods of justifying her position. But this does not explain why Amenhotep III (and later also Ramesses II, in some less substantial surviving scenes) should have felt the need to utilize the myth of divine birth when none of Hatshepsut's 'gender problems' applied. In *The Miraculous Birth of King Amon-hotep III and Other Egyptian Studies* (1912) Colin Campbell argued that the reasons for the birth scenes of both Hatshepsut and Amenhotep III were essentially religious rather than political, being concerned with the replacement of the cult of Ra in the kingship by that of Amun, so that the aim was to establish the king as the son of Amun rather than the son of the sun-god Ra. It has been pointed out, however, that Amun was already being described as the king's father as early as the reign of Ahmose, three generations before Hatshepsut. Essentially the question of Hatshepsut's motivation for stressing her divine birth remains uncertain.

Although patchy data can always lead to interpretive problems, there can be little doubt that these three problems with 20th-century interpretations of the reign of Hatshepsut derive at least partly from Egyptologists' assumptions and personal prejudices, which cause them not only to interpret the evidence in misleading ways but to blatantly build up semi-fictionalized images of the female ruler, no doubt bringing to the topic a wide range of (largely inappropriate) later female royal stereotypes from Western history, such as Elizabeth I and Victoria. When Michael Rice, for instance, speculates about Hatshepsut's possible relationship with Senenmut he draws on Russian history:

> She seems to have maintained some sort of intimate relationship with her architect Senenmut, who may have been the father of her daughter Neferure; perhaps he played Potemkin to her Catherine, whom she considerably resembled.

Apart from Hatshepsut, two other Egyptian 'queens' to receive the full treatment in posthumous personality profiling are Nefertiti (one of whose sculptures has become a kind of celebrity in its own right) and Cleopatra VII, the last of the Ptolemaic rulers and one of the foremost cultural icons of the movie industry during the 20th century. I will discuss the reputations and multifarious influences of Nefertiti and Cleopatra in the last chapter of this book, since these two Egyptian queens have undoubtedly crossed over into the arena of modern popular culture.

Ramesses the Great

A considerably more conventional – but nevertheless still stereotyped – view of Egyptian kingship is encountered in the case of Ramesses II, who seems to have begun to be regarded as some kind of archetype even before he died. During the last years of his reign he had become a living legend and was evidently much admired (and envied) by his successors, such as Ramesses III, who, only 30 years after his more illustrious predecessor's death, not only dedicated a chapel to the deified Ramesses II at Medinet Habu, but also gave his own sons the same names as Ramesses II's sons.

By the 11th century BC Ramesses had become such a potent mythological figure that one magical papyrus evidently expected to gain extra potency by identifying itself as 'the writing which was found on the neck of the mummy of King Usimare (Ramesses II)'. It is also clear that Ramesses had become very closely associated with the institution of Egyptian kingship itself from the fact that, in the Third Intermediate Period, priests and high officials were sometimes given the title: 'King's son of Ramesses', showing the great power of the name Ramesses alone.

Ramesses II's memory would live on in later traditions both under his own name and under that of Sesostris, in reality the name of several Middle Kingdom rulers whose monuments he had avidly usurped during his lifetime, and whose reputations were also inexorably absorbed into his own. In the 5th century, Herodotus described a character called Rhampsinitus, whom he credits with the building of the gateways at the western end of the precinct of Ptah at Memphis, also suggesting that he was a frequent visitor to the underworld. In his *Histories* 2. 121–3, Herodotus describes two events in the reign of Rhampsinitus, who seems to be a semi-mythologized mixture of Ramesses II and III. The first is an account of how the king went to play dice in the underworld, while the second tells of a cunning theft from the king's treasury and his attempts to thwart the thieves.

About 400 years later, in the early 1st century BC, Diodorus Siculus quotes Hecataeus of Abdera in describing the tomb of Osymandias, which appears to be the Ramesseum, Ramesses II's mortuary temple. The name Osymandias was a Hellenization of User-maat-ra, Ramesses II's prenomen. Diodorus gives an account of Osymandias' supposed war against the 'Bactrians', which seems to be a distant memory of the genuine historical war against the Hittites, including the battle of Qadesh. Diodorus provided a paraphrased version of Hecataeus of Abdera's description of the colossal statues of the king in the Ramesseum:

> Beside the entrance to the temple are three statues, each carved from a single block of black stone from Syene. One of these, which is seated, is the largest of any in Egypt . . . The inscription on it runs: 'King of kings I am, Osymandias. If anyone would know how great I am and where I lie, let him surpass my works'.

If this discussion of statues and the hubris of despotic rulers seems a little remote from the modern world, we need only look back as far as war in Iraq in 2003, when televisions around the world showed the toppling of one of Saddam Hussein's colossal statues as the consummate symbol of his regime's defeat.

Diodorus' 'Bactrian' theme is picked up in an inscribed slab known as the Bentresh Stele (now in the Louvre), which was an inscription composed sometime between the 4th and 2nd centuries BC, although purporting to date from the reign of Ramesses II (1290–1224). This black sandstone stele was found at Karnak in a small Ptolemaic sanctuary near the temple of Khonsu. The text claims that the king married a foreign princess called Neferura, from the land of Bakhtan (Bactria?), whose sister falls gravely ill. A manifestation of the god Khonsu, known as 'the provider', is credited with the ability to drive out evil spirits. Ramesses is therefore said to have sent a statue of Khonsu to his Syrian father-in-law in order to facilitate the cure of Neferura's ailing sister called Bentresh. There may be some distant echoes here of Ramesses' actual marriage to a Hittite princess, since she was given the name of Ma-hor-neferura, which is fairly similar to that of the foreign princess in the Bentresh Stele. We do not know what propagandist purpose was served by this stele – was it intended to glorify the role of Khonsu as a merciful and beneficent deity (*pa ir sekher*: 'the maker of plans' or 'the provider')? Was it to resolve a rivalry between the priesthoods of the two main forms of Khonsu? Or was it to recall national glory *vis-à-vis* the outside world at a time of national weakness? The one thing that is certain is that the reign of Ramesses II, like that of Sneferu in the Old Kingdom, had come to be regarded by the Egyptians as a kind of timeless golden age.

Nevertheless, Ramesses' reputation received another dose of negative spin-doctoring in 1817, when Percy Bysshe Shelley published a sonnet called 'Ozymandias' that included the famous lines:

> 'My name is Ozymandias, king of kings:
> look on my works ye mighty, and despair!'
> Nothing besides remains. Round the decay
> Of that colossal wreck, boundless and bare
> The lone and level sands stretch far away.

Shelley in fact never visited Egypt and was probably inspired by visits to the British Museum, since we know that he was in London in 1817, and in fact a few months before he wrote the Ozymandias sonnet he had spent an evening with Keats and Leigh Hunt writing poems about the River Nile. The poem has a clear debt to Diodorus Siculus, and Shelley had presumably also read William Hamilton's guidebook to Egypt, *Aegyptiaca*, which was published in 1809. It is also probably significant that it was in 1817 that the British Museum received part of a colossal statue of Ramesses called the Younger Memnon, brought back from the second court of the Ramesseum by Belzoni as a gift from Mohammed Ali to the Prince Regent.

Even the ethnicity of Ramesses has been the subject of discussion.

As we shall see in Chapter 6 (which deals, among other things, with the racial and ethnic identity of the Egyptians) there have been many Egyptologists with racist and ethnocentric axes to grind over the years. One of these was the so-called 'hyper-diffusionist', Sir Grafton Elliot Smith, whose examination of the mummies of Seti I, Ramesses II, and Merenptah led him to argue that they each had 'many more alien [Asiatic] traits in face and cranium', suggesting that they were 'less characteristically Egyptian' compared with the 18th-Dynasty rulers. Given his racist views, there seems little doubt that he was keen to establish that these heroic warrior-kings were non-African in origin. According to Bruce Trigger, Smith and his fellow-diffusionists believed that 'most human beings are naturally primitive and will always revert to a stage of savagery if not stopped from doing so by the ruling classes'. It was therefore perhaps considered to be essential that Ramesses and the rest of his family be shown to be racially distinct from their subjects in order to conform to the idea of 'ruling' and 'subject' races respectively.

Ramesses has of course also enjoyed something of a fictional afterlife, with a sequence of novels written about him by the Egyptologist-turned-writer Christian Jacq, as well as (in 1989) a book by Ann Rice, called *The Mummy or Ramesses the Damned*, in which Ramesses is resurrected by a magic elixir (along with Cleopatra).

As we saw earlier in this chapter, the reputation of Hatshepsut was very much formed by modern Egyptologists' sense that she was an anomaly and that she needed to have her own special narrative, whether the solid evidence for this was actually there or not. In contrast, the approach to Ramesses II, from the late New Kingdom through to 20th-century accounts of his life and reign, seems to have been to allow him to serve as a kind of amalgam of the classic traits of arrogance and despotism that tend to be regarded as appropriate to Egyptian kingship. Consequently, when the Victorian novelist and founder of the Egypt Exploration Society, Amelia Edwards, wrote about Ramesses in 1877, she described him as 'ruthless in war, prodigal in peace, rapacious of booty, and unsparing in the exercise of almost boundless power', not because she had necessarily scoured the available evidence to build up this vivid portrait, but because she evidently took at face value the stereotype presented to us from at least Hecataeus onwards.

Finally, one of Ramesses' most even-handed biographers, Kenneth Kitchen, attempts to protect Ramesses from such careless type-casting, but in the process seems to create a rather genial monarch. Criticizing his fellow Egyptologists for their Amelia-Edwards-style pigeonholing of Ramesses, he speculates as to what the king would make of the modern world:

> Initially, perhaps, he would be dazzled by the technology and sciences . . . But before very long he would see through the material façade and (in quest of Maat) perceive also the reverse of the coin in a world cursed with exactly the same basic human rivalries and failings that he knew in his own world . . . Finally he would doubtless also see the abiding positive values of love, devotion, regard for right, a certain mutual tolerance on non-essentials . . .

If the Hecateus/Edwards despotic view of Ramesses is disturbing, then how much more disturbing is the Kitchenized concept of Ramesses as the archbishop of Canterbury.

For a genuine dose of realism on the stereotypes of Egyptian kingship, we should perhaps turn to Jan Assman, who (in *The Search for God in Ancient Egypt*) describes the way in which kingship seems to lie at the heart of Egyptian creation myths:

> The starting point was the king. He was the incarnation of the god Horus, the son who ever and again has to overcome the death of his father to gain his throne. The Ennead [group of nine creation deities] before whom he must prove that he is the rightful heir to the throne is both his family and the cosmos itself; read in descending order, his genealogy is a cosmogony. Therein lies the legitimacy of

his office: it is the rule that the primeval god had exercised over those who emerged from him, the office of Atum, which had passed through the cosmogonic succession of the gods of air and earth to Osiris, the deceased father, and from him to the succession of historical kings in whom his son Horus was incarnate.

This passage gives some sense of the context of most of the texts and images that have survived from the reigns of Amenhotep II, Hatshepsut, and Ramesses II, and with all this cosmic imagery, we should be grateful that we can catch any faint glimpses of individuality and personality from the sources. If Egyptian rulers sound arrogant, this is because they were obliged to see themselves, at least in theory, as the lynchpins of humanity and the universe.

Chapter 6
Identity: issues of ethnicity, race, and gender

The Narmer Palette includes scenes in which either the king
himself or his divine alter-egos (the falcon-god Horus on one side
and a bull on the other) dispatch or humiliate foreigners and
enemies. As we have seen above, these images are part of the
paraphernalia of Egyptian stereotypical kingship, but they are also
part of the iconography through which the Egyptians defined and
reaffirmed themselves as a people and as a nation, in contrast to the
chaotic sea of foreignness that lay beyond their borders. We might
ask, however, whether the figure held in captivity by the Horus
falcon was a Libyan or Asiatic, or whether this was still a case of
civil war and the prisoner is a Lower Egyptian, in the process of
being forcibly integrated into an Upper Egyptian kingdom. We
might also ask whether the two prone figures in the lower part of
the palette, and also decapitated human figures on the other
side of the palette, are Lower Egyptians or foreigners. Did Upper
Egyptians regard Lower Egyptians as quasi-foreigners at this date?
Were the king and his courtiers not 'Egyptian' themselves but

invaders from the Near East, as Egyptologists such as Petrie and Emery argued? If so, which figures on the palette were the true Egyptians?

The iconography of Egypt's early ethnic identity

It seems in fact that the Narmer Palette may have a particular significance with regard to the early pharaonic Egyptians' definition of their own national identity. Toby Wilkinson argues that Narmer is the last ruler to be depicted as an animated version of the creature contained in his name: hence Narmer's ivory label and cylinder (see Chapter 3) both show the somewhat improbably anthropomorphized catfish in the act of smiting foreign captives, whereas the palette bears not only the bestial symbols of pharaoh as falcon and bull, but also the image of the smiting human figure of the king. Wilkinson therefore suggests that

> The Narmer Palette is . . . a striking amalgam of earlier and later conventions of royal iconography. Narmer's reign marked a defining transition in the concept of rule; nowhere is this better exemplified than on his palette.

He also argues that the palette is probably the last royal artefact to be decorated with a borrowed Mesopotamian motif (the serpopards entwined around the palette's central depression) and that therefore

> As Egypt's rulers rejected royal iconography and turned instead to indigenous motifs, so too the official ideology towards the outside world underwent a profound change at the beginning of the First Dynasty . . . State ideology henceforth characterised non-Egyptians as the human equivalents of untamed wild beasts, standing outside the Egyptian realm and therefore hostile to Egypt, its king, its people and its way of life.

Questions of identity undoubtedly pervade the Narmer Palette just as they permeate the subject of Egyptology as a whole. What was it like to be an ancient Egyptian, and how did they distinguish themselves from neighbouring peoples? Were they a black African civilization or one of several variants of standard Near Eastern culture? Should we define them by their language, their geographical location, or their physical appearance? How did they see themselves? In many ways the Egyptians defined themselves and their rulers by establishing and emphasizing sharp contrasts with non-Egyptians in Africa and the Near East. The regions with which Egypt gradually fostered commercial and political links can be grouped into three basic areas: Africa (primarily Nubia, Libya, and Punt), Asia (Syria–Palestine, Mesopotamia, Arabia, and Anatolia), and the northern and eastern Mediterranean (Cyprus, Crete, the Sea Peoples, and the Greeks).

The Narmer Palette may also have something to say about early Egyptian contact with the outside world. As long ago as 1955, an analysis by the Israeli archaeologist Yigael Yadin led to the suggestion that the Narmer Palette might not simply be a series of scenes celebrating kingly power or ritual, nor even, as the older theories suggested, a narrative of the unification of Egypt. Instead, Yadin argued that it might show early Egyptian military conflict with the Near East. He focused on the two prone figures below the large smiting figure of King Narmer. As I noted in Chapter 1, these two figures appear to be identified in some way by a pair of hieroglyph-like signs. The left-hand sign seems to be the rectangular outline of a fortified enclosure, while the right-hand one, if it is also an architectural image, might be seen as a semi-circular enclosure with two walls fanning out from it. Yadin suggests that this right-hand sign might be the Egyptians' rendition of a peculiar kite-shaped enclosure (i.e. diamond-shaped, with a pair of hanging 'strings', when viewed from above), many examples of which have survived in the Hamad desert near the modern city of Amman, where they are thought to have served as fortified enclosures into which animals could be herded in order to protect them from raiding parties. These two signs may therefore identify the places of origin of the two figures, and if Yadin is correct, the first may represent the fortified enclosures that might have been encountered by Egyptians campaigning in Early Bronze Age Palestine, and the second may portray the kite-like enclosures associated with the nomadic pastoralists of the Trans-Jordanian region.

Interestingly enough, excavations at the Silo Site in the Nahal Tillah region of Israel during the 1990s have revealed an Egyptian potsherd bearing the name of Narmer written in a *serekh* frame, along with many other Egyptian artefacts, including prestige items such as mace-heads, of similar date. This, together with evidence for substantial Egyptian activity at Tel Erani, to the north-west of Nahal Tillah, suggests that there was certainly a strong Egyptian presence in Palestine, which might therefore provide some archaeological support for Yadin's theory of very early Egyptian military expansion into the Levant.

Black Egyptians: Bernal, Diop, and the reinvention of Kemet

I cannot leave the subject of the identity of the Egyptians as a nation without attempting to tackle the very contemporary question of the extent to which the ancient Egyptians should be regarded as racially and ethnically 'black'. How justified are such writers as Martin Bernal and Cheikh Anta Diop in regarding Egypt as an essentially 'black' civilization culturally appropriated and misrepresented by white Europeans? In 1981 Diop confidently asserted that 'Egyptians were Negroes, thick-lipped, kinky-haired and thin-legged'. Although it is certainly true that *some* surviving Egyptian mummies or depictions of ancient Egyptians fit this description, the fact is that most of both the former and the latter are anthropologically and visually quite different to Diop's description.

How did the Egyptians view themselves? We can answer this question first by looking at the way in which they portrayed themselves in painting and sculpture, and second by analysing their depictions of 'foreigners'. As in many other cultures, the Egyptians seem to have gained a sense of their own identity primarily by contrasting themselves with the peoples of the world outside Egypt. The iconography of the Egyptians' depictions of themselves and foreigners suggests that, for most of their history, they saw themselves as midway between the black, woolly-haired Africans and the pale, bearded Asiatics. Scenes in the tombs of the New Kingdom pharaohs Seti I and Ramesses III in the Valley of the Kings specifically depict the various human types in the universe over which the sun-god Ra presided. These types included reddish-brown Egyptians whose skin colour contrasts equally starkly both with the black-skinned Kushites (Nubians) and with the paler-skinned Libyans and Asiatics. Although partly based on skin colour and other physical characteristics, these ancient ethnic types were also based on varieties in hairstyles and costume, and their function was apparently to allow the Egyptians to define themselves as a national group, relative to the rest of the world. Such depictions, however, would have been recognized by the Egyptians themselves as simplified stereotypes, given that the thousands of portrayals of individual Egyptians show that the population as a whole ranged across a wide spectrum of complexions, from light to dark brown and black.

There is, therefore, also a sense in which the 'Egyptians' regarded themselves as a distinct population in purely *cultural* non-racial terms. There are many examples of individuals whom Egyptians regarded as identical to themselves in social and political terms, despite the fact that they were obviously 'foreign' in their physical appearance. One good example of this is Maiherpri, a military official in the early 18th Dynasty who was granted the great privilege of a tomb in the Valley of the Kings but whose physical features (very dark complexion and curly hair) clearly indicate that he was of Nubian extraction. On the Asiatic side, a man called Aper-el, whose name indicates his Near Eastern roots, rose to the rank of vizier (the highest civil office below that of the king himself) in the late 18th Dynasty, and there were many other Asiatics who gained powerful positions among the Egyptian elite at this date.

Egyptologists, particularly in North America, cannot escape the fact that ancient Egyptian culture has become a 'black issue'. The view that Egypt was a fundamentally black civilization – often described as an 'Afrocentric' position – is important to many Africans and African Americans because it gives both Africans and black people a much more significant stake in the emergence of early civilizations. Many Afrocentrists regard the standard Egyptological study of 'Egypt' as so tainted that they will only refer to the country by the ancient Egyptian toponym Kemet (literally 'the black land', although in actual fact this term refers to the black fertile soil rather than the colour of the people). A wide spectrum of Afrocentrist arguments have been advanced, ranging from the highly intellectual thesis of Martin Bernal, some of whose arguments in the two volumes of *Black Athena* present a convincing case for regarding Egypt as an important stimulus for 'Western' civilization, via the considerably more tenuous and polemical assertions of Cheikh Anta Diop (e.g. 'the "pope" of the Yoruba, the Oni, has the same title as Osiris, the Egyptian god'), to the downright emotive or obscure, such as Molefi Kete Asante's suggestion that

> ... the *mdw ntr*, the written text, came to represent the entire African universe. Each glyph was itself a small part of the universe, and thus writing as the materialization of thought was repeated throughout the African continent with sculpture as the making substance of thought.

There is no doubt that some Egyptologists in the past have been guilty of racist interpretations of the Egyptians. At the most heinous end of the scale, Grafton Elliot Smith suggested in 1909 that 'the smallest infusion of Negro-blood immediately manifests itself in a dulling of initiative and a "drag" on the further development of the arts of civilisation'. It is also difficult to read the theories advanced by Flinders Petrie concerning the establishment of pharaonic Egypt by an invading Near Eastern or even European 'master-race' without being aware of his right-wing political views (he wrote a pamphlet on the dangers of socialism) and the fact that he was an enthusiastic member of the eugenics movement, which was dedicated to 'improving' human stock by 'the study of agencies under social control that may improve or impair the racial qualities of future generations' (according to its founder, the anthopologist Sir Francis Galton). Bryan Emery's espousal of invasion theories concerning early Egypt, on the other hand, was no doubt influenced more by the diffusionist ideas of Gordon Childe, but also perhaps by pre-war British colonialism in Egypt and the Sudan.

However, to assume, as many Afrocentrists appear to do, first that much conventional Egyptological thought is still infected by such racism, and second that the very existence of such prejudice in some way proves that, contrary to much of the visual and written evidence, ancient Egyptians were both black and African, seems a little unjustified. Perhaps the last word on this should be left to C. Loring Brace:

> The 'race' concept did not exist in Egypt, and it is not mentioned in Herodotus, the Bible, or any of the other writings of classical antiquity. Because it has neither biological nor social justification, we should strive to see that it is eliminated from both public and private usage. Its absence will be missed by no one, and we shall all be better off without it. R.I.P.

Gender and sexuality

Questions of Egyptian identity have occupied Egyptologists for almost as long as the subject has existed, but there are some aspects of identity that have been less frequently addressed, probably because Egyptologists have tended to be white European or North American male academics. The heads of the goddess Bat at the top of the Narmer Palette appear to be the only female elements of the palette's decoration (and one Egyptologist, the art historian

Whitney Davis, has argued that even these may actually be the heads of a bull-god). The palette, like the majority of Egyptian art and texts, is essentially a male-dominated artefact. This raises the question of what we know of women in ancient Egypt, and indeed what we know of the Egyptians' own views on gender and sexuality. Which aspects of Egyptian society were overtly or implicitly moulded by male or female concerns?

When we look at the patterning of gender in Egyptian textual and visual sources, it is almost immediately apparent that male images and concerns are much more frequent and prominent than those of women. This male skew in the data occurs in a number of different ways, some obvious and others much more subtle and insidious. As we have seen with the summary of views of Queen Hatshepsut's reign, very few women reached the office of ruler during almost three millennia of the pharaonic period. In tomb chapels, women are regularly secondary figures, since the tombs were nearly always intended primarily for their fathers, husbands, or sons. In its texts and artistic iconography Egypt was androcentric from at least the 1st Dynasty onwards. This is partly a false impression conveyed by our biased selection of data, but it was also, in some respects, how it actually was in Egyptian society, with virtually all women being illiterate, often excluded from administration, and generally invisible in the world of work, with the notable exception of textile production, brewing, and baking (although men are also shown engaged in the two latter activities). Tomb paintings and wooden funerary models regularly show women spinning and weaving, and sometimes harvesting flax in agricultural scenes, and some texts indicate that this was one of the main activities in the royal harem (a fact which seems to have escaped many Victorian Orientalist painters when they were evoking scenes of 'pharaoh's harem').

In the past, the mainly male scholars of Egyptology simply took this situation for granted, making little effort to 'unpick' the roles and lifeways of women from this male-oriented documentation. In the

15. Scene in a Deir el-Medina tomb-chapel, 20th Dynasty, c.1160 BC.

last 30 years, however, as the numbers of female professional Egyptologists have increased, so, not surprisingly, more attempts have been made to read between the lines in search of evidence for women's lives and achievements. It has become apparent, for instance, that the situation changed over time, so that there were actually three phases of the pharaonic period when women were more prominent in the documentation: in the Old Kingdom, when they were allowed to hold some administrative posts (although only being placed in charge of groups of women); in the early 18th Dynasty, when women are more frequently featured on funerary monuments, probably reflecting their greater ability to take part in funerary rituals; and in the period from the late 20th to the early 22nd Dynasty, when they not only again appear more often in tomb chapels but are also increasingly shown without any of their male relatives in attendance.

Inevitably perhaps – given Egyptology's long-standing predisposition for elite monuments – much of the early work concentrated on the study of royal and elite women such as Hetepheres (the mother of Khufu), Sobekneferu (a female ruler at the end of the 12th Dynasty), Hatshepsut, and Nefertiti. Gradually, however, greater effort has been applied to the extraction of information on women of all classes and wealth-levels, and this shift of focus has been greatly assisted and encouraged by the tendency of newly favoured settlement archaeology to produce the kind of objective socio-economic evidence that at least has the potential to reveal the more female-oriented aspects of Egypt. Those parts of domestic and public life that male documents and artistic images can render invisible are sometimes considerably more obvious in the archaeological record. A note of caution, however, needs to be sounded when it comes to analysing houses for patterns of use by different genders, since it would be all too easy to make unwarranted ethnocentric assumptions concerning male and female space (e.g. women/kitchen, men/reception room, women/bedroom).

Another area of gender studies in which Egyptologists have often been guilty of ethnocentricity is in the delicate area of sexuality. In Chapter 8, below, I discuss the fact that Egyptian religion includes an explicit focus on the phalluses of certain deities. Many Egyptologists, brought up almost entirely in the Judaeo-Christian religious traditions, have, academically speaking, averted their eyes from this phallocentrism, regarding it, consciously or subconsciously, as somehow inappropriate in a religious context. Broadly speaking, this led many scholars to attempt to downplay such episodes as the description of Atum's act of masturbation in order to create the next generation of deities (in the absence of any goddess with which to procreate). In Raymond Faulkner's translation, Pyramid Text 527 unequivocally states:

> Atum is he who once came into being, who masturbated in On [Heliopolis]. He took his phallus in his grasp that he might create orgasm by means of it, and so were born, Shu and Tefnut.

However, Wallis Budge, the Keeper of Egyptian and Assyrian Antiquities at the British Museum from 1892 to 1924, referred to this mythical act as 'a brutal example of naturalism', which he can evidently only explain by assuming it to be some kind of survival from prehistoric religion, while the American Egyptologist James Henry Breasted obliquely translates the text with the phrase 'by his own masculine power, self-developed', making no real reference to the sexual act at all.

Only two books have so far been written on sex in pharaonic and Greco-Roman Egypt, but one characteristic Egyptological assumption that both authors highlight is the conventional tendency to assign sexually related artefacts and images to the more anodyne area of 'fertility' rather than acknowledging overtly sexual images and activities. As Lynn Meskell has put it,

> Women's sexuality, not their fertility (i.e. pregnancy), is stressed in tomb scenes, and their sexual qualities were presumably a sought

after commodity in the afterlife as were provisions of servants and food.

Tom Hare, however, points out more cautiously that it may often be difficult to decide when representations are actually intended to be erotic or not:

> However attractive we may find the painting of a bare-breasted Egyptian woman or goddess, we would be rash to read into this an erotic interest beyond our own personal interest. This is because in formal canonical representation, adult women and goddesses are often depicted bare-breasted, with the nipple of the forward breast delineated.

He goes on to discuss the complexity of the picture we are presented with, given that statues show women in particular types of dress which in this context conceal the breasts, and yet the same dresses in two-dimensional depictions may show one of the breasts – this appears to be some kind of artistic convention rather than eroticization. On the other hand, he accepts that there is almost certainly deliberate sexuality observable in the appearance, in mid-18th Dynasty elite tombs, of fully nude female dancers, musicians, and servants, and therefore suggests that, in these contexts, 'the female figure is clearly the object of the male subject's gaze'.

The net result of these discussions of ethnicity, race, gender, and sexuality in ancient Egypt is to show that these are surely among the most controversial and fascinating areas of current Egyptological research. Since the modern Western world itself is deeply immersed in such identity crises, from 'political correctness' to 'ethnic cleansing' and 'race hate', it is hardly surprising that ancient Egyptian source material has become fresh grist to these mills (a phrase unintentionally reminiscent of the way in which Manchester mill-owners are rumoured, probably slanderously, to have used Egyptian mummies as fuel . . .).

Chapter 7

Death: mummification, dismemberment, and the cult of Osiris

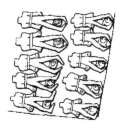

Although the Narmer Palette and the Narmer mace-head, two of the most significant artefacts from this king's reign, were both discovered at Hierakonpolis, his burial seems to have been located alongside those of the other rulers of Dynasties 0 and 1, in Cemetery B, at the site of Umm el-Qa'ab in Abydos, 150 km to the north-west of Hierakonpolis. The double-chamber tomb B17/18 has been identified as the likely resting place of Narmer, although the actual textual evidence associating it with him is fairly slim. Also in Cemetery B are the tombs of Narmer's 1st-Dynasty successor Aha, and his two likely predecessors, Iri-Hor and Ka (although some scholars argue that these are not the names of two specific 'Dynasty 0' kings, but instead are simply general royal epithets that might apply to any of the late Predynastic or 1st-Dynasty rulers, or even specifically to different aspects of Narmer, in which case these four other chambers might be additional parts of Narmer's funerary complex). The tombs of Iri-Hor, Ka, and Narmer all consist of double chambers, whereas that of Aha is a funerary complex made up of several separate chambers, which were built in three stages. Aha's tomb also contains a new ingredient: 33 subsidiary burials to the north-east of his complex, containing the remains of young men, each 20–5 years old, who were probably killed when the king was buried. In addition, close to one of these subsidiary graves, the excavations have revealed the remains of at least seven young lions, perhaps buried as symbols of royal identification with the lion.

It is in fact a slightly later 1st-Dynasty tomb at Abydos – the burial of Aha's successor Djer (perhaps Narmer's grandson) – that is most relevant to the subject of this chapter: the cult of Osiris and Egyptian attitudes to the dead. Djer's tomb (covering an area of 70 x 40 metres, including the subsidiary burials in rows) was the largest in the Early Dynastic royal cemetery at Abydos, and it was here that Flinders Petrie found part of a linen-wrapped arm wearing precious bracelets hidden in the north wall of the tomb (and therefore saved when the tomb was burnt in ancient times). This may be the one surviving fragment of an actual royal body in the Early Dynastic cemetery as a whole, although sadly only the jewellery and a few of the linen bandages survive today (the former in the Egyptian Museum, Cairo, and the latter in the Petrie Museum, University College London), removing any real possibility of the limb being scientifically dated to establish or refute its contemporaneity with Djer.

By the Middle Kingdom, if not earlier, the tomb of Djer had been converted into a cenotaph (literally 'empty tomb') of the god Osiris, thus transforming it into a centre of 'pilgrimage' containing a stone image of the god, which was discovered still in place when the French archaeologist Emile Amélineau first excavated the burial in 1897. The tomb seems to have eventually been regarded as the ultimate, quintessential royal funerary memorial: the mythical burial place of the god Osiris, whose entire religious cult was intimately connected with the concept of the dead king. So who or what was Osiris, and why is he so important to our understanding of death, mummies, and all the rest?

'Foremost of the westerners'

Osiris, the god of the dead and the afterlife, is one of the earliest in the Egyptian pantheon, probably starting off as a fertility god linked with agriculture, and perhaps also the Nile 'inundation'. Like many other major deities, he gradually acquired the attributes of other gods as his worship spread throughout the country. At some point he arrived at Abydos, where he took on the epithet Khenty-imentiu ('foremost of the westerners'), which was the name of an earlier jackal-form god of the dead worshipped there. From at least the Middle Kingdom onwards, an annual festival of Osiris took place at Abydos, involving the procession of the god in his *neshmet* boat, preceded by the jackal-god Wepwawet ('opener of the way'). Scenes from Osiris' triumph over his enemies were acted out in this procession, before the god was returned to his sanctuary for purification. The rites connected with the 'mysteries' of Osiris were enacted in the temple, probably celebrating his original connection with fertility. Some aspects of these Osirian rituals are mentioned on a stele (now in the Berlin Museum) that was set up at Abydos by a priest called Ikhernofret, evidently the organizer of the annual festival in the time of the 12th-Dynasty ruler Senusret III.

At a fairly early stage Osiris seems to have taken over the insignia of the god Andjety, from whom he also probably took the mythical attribute of deity as dead ruler. Andjety's cult centre Djedu, in the Delta, therefore later became known as Busiris, and was said to be the place identified with Osiris' backbone (the symbol of which was the *djed*-pillar). The combination of his associations with fertility and death almost inevitably ensured that Osiris became the ultimate god of resurrection, and the link with the dead king was established by the 5th Dynasty at the latest. It became essential for

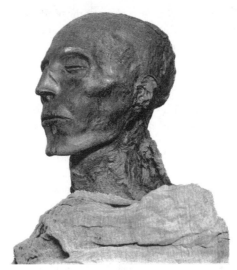

16. The mummified head of Seti I, 19th Dynasty, *c.*1300 BC.

the mummified body to be associated with Osiris in order to gain eternal life.

Egyptian texts have a tendency to allude to various divine myths through references to rituals and the use of various epithets, but their literature is notoriously lacking in straightforward narrative-style myths. Reconstructing Egyptian mythology from ancient Egyptian texts can be rather like piecing together the biblical account of the birth of Jesus from a series of Christmas cards and carols. Consequently, the myths associated with Osiris are best known not from an Egyptian source but from a much later compilation of the legend by the Greek writer Plutarch (AD *c.*46–126). Some elements of Plutarch's version have been corroborated by surviving fragments of the stories in Egyptian sources, but others may possibly be Greek or Roman inventions. He describes Osiris as a human ruler whose accidental(!) adultery with his sister-in-law Nephthys caused his evil brother Seth to become jealous and to plot secretly against him. Seth discovered the measurements of his brother's body and had a magnificent casket made to fit him. He next organized a banquet to which he invited 72 accomplices as well as Osiris. During the feast he brought forward the chest and declared that whoever fitted it exactly should have it as a gift. Having stepped into the coffin, Osiris was locked inside and the lid was sealed with molten lead. The coffin was then thrown into the Nile and eventually drifted down to the Mediterranean, washing up at the Syrian port of Byblos. This city always had strong links with ancient Egypt, particularly through the supply of cedar-wood, therefore it is perhaps no surprise that the coffin is then said to have become entangled in a cedar tree.

His wife Isis eventually rescues Osiris and returns to Egypt, hiding him in his coffin in the marshes prior to giving him a decent burial. However, Seth is said to have stumbled on the casket and angrily dismembered the body of his brother, scattering the body-parts (their number varies in different accounts, from 14 to 42) throughout Egypt. Isis searches for the body-parts and buries each at the place where it is found. Plutarch's version of the story claims that the phallus was eaten by the Nile carp (*Lepidotus*), the *Phagrus* and the *Oxyrynchus* fish, so that an artificial penis had to be manufactured, but it is noticeable that none of the fragmentary Egyptian accounts suggest this, since the fertile phallus was a crucial element in the cult. The original Egyptian versions also add another episode after Osiris's dismembered body was reassembled into the form of the first mummy – they describe how Isis was impregnated by the mummified body, and conceived the child Horus. This moment of conception is portrayed in a scene showing Isis in the form of a kite hovering on the mummy's penis. Versions of this scene have been found both in the shrine of Sokar–Osiris in the temple of Seti I at Abydos and also in one of the roof chambers of the temple of Hathor at Dendera.

Many of the principal features of the myth of Osiris and Isis are already attested by the Old Kingdom (2686–2160), including his death by drowning, and the discovery of his body by Isis. The identification of Seth, the god of the desert and chaos, as his murderer was in place by the Middle Kingdom (2040–1640), although the story doesn't yet explicitly refer to his dismemberment of the dead Osiris. It is the process of dismemberment, however, that provides the most telling insights into Egyptian culture. We can rarely be sure whether myths reflect ritual or inspire it, or whether other kinds of processes lie behind the surviving texts and images, but there seems to be a web of links between the myth of Osiris and the process of mummification. Herodotus's very detailed account of Egyptian mummification describes the main practitioners as *paraschistai* ('slitters') and *taricheutai* ('picklers'), and, although the terms are somewhat irreverent, they convey well the two principal stages: the body must first be cut up and to some extent dismembered by the slitters before it can be reassembled and preserved by the picklers. The Osiris myth is therefore a very accurate prototype for the practical process of physical preservation.

Although the cult of Osiris permeates the Egyptians' funerary beliefs in various forms, there are probably two particular aspects of the cult that are most prominent and influential. The first of these is the way in which, by the New Kingdom, it became increasingly common for funerary texts to make explicit connections between the deceased and Osiris, and for the descriptions of the fate of any dead individual to deliberately echo parts of the myth. The second is the significance of the site of Abydos as a focus of private funerary cults. The survival of large numbers of private funerary stelae and cenotaphs dedicated at Abydos by private individuals shows that the cult of Osiris became extremely popular (in the literal sense of the word) from at least as early as the end of the Old Kingdom. Even when individuals were unable to place stelae or monuments at Abydos itself, they incorporated items or images in their tombs that refer to the act of making a pilgrimage to Abydos, as in the case of boat models, which sometimes symbolized the voyage of the body of the deceased to the home of Osiris. The idea of the *Abydosfahrt* (described by Egyptians as a 'voyage in peace'), an imaginary journey to Abydos, first appeared in the Middle Kingdom in the tombs of the local governors Amenemhet and Khnumhotep II, taking the form of painted scenes showing boats sailing to and from the cult-place, while the texts describe the deceased man's participation in the festival of Osiris.

By the late Middle Kingdom the creation of private funerary monuments at Abydos had evidently already become so prevalent that the 13th-Dynasty ruler Wegaf issued a decree forbidding tombs to be built on the processional way. The expansion of Osirid funerary privileges beyond the immediate sphere of the royal family was once famously (and rather inaccurately) described by the American Egyptologist John Wilson as the 'democratization of the afterlife': in other words, the extension of once-royal funerary privileges to ordinary people, allowing them to physically take part in the rites of Osiris and thus acquire funerary benefits that had previously been restricted to kings. The use of the term 'democratization' inevitably suggests some kind of erosion of belief in the kingship as a direct result of the usurping of royal formulae and rituals, but it has been pointed out that, on the contrary, the act of imitation might actually be taken to imply a strengthening belief in the effectiveness of the institution of kingship.

Ancient Egyptian attitudes to death

The old cliché that Egyptians were totally obsessed with death is in danger of being eclipsed by a new cliché, since many recent books have made the point that their tombs contain ample evidence that they were actually obsessed with *life*, in the form of endless 'daily life' scenes and models, depicting individuals working in the fields, making wine, banqueting, playing music, dancing, and numerous other life-affirming activities. In reality, if we are going to caricature the Egyptians, there are good grounds for assuming that their real concerns lay somewhere between these two extremes. Certainly in the elite sphere of society they devoted more of their time and financial resources to preparations for death than we would necessarily consider healthy, but it is equally certain that our view of their society has always been disproportionately biased towards the funerary side of things, partly because cemeteries and other funerary phenomena were invariably placed in the desert and have therefore been much better preserved than their houses, towns, and marketplaces, most of which were located in wetter conditions closer to the Nile or other sources of water (and have also tended to be covered by modern towns and cities). The fact that so much of our excavated evidence relates to death and the afterlife is also a direct result of many Egyptologists' own preference for data relating to these topics, which means that until recently many research agendas were geared towards funerary or religious matters rather than social or economic trends, although, as we saw at the end of Chapter 1, this situation has changed significantly in recent decades, with more research projects focusing on the survey and excavation of towns and cities. Nevertheless, the vast majority of Egyptological evidence is still oriented more towards death than life.

The ancient Egyptians' attitudes to life and death were heavily influenced by their steadfast belief that eternal life could be ensured by a wide range of strategies, including piety to the gods, the preservation of the body through mummification, and the provision of statuary and other funerary equipment. In modern terms this might be described as a scattergun technique, and the survival of numerous tombs and funerary texts has enabled Egyptologists to explore the complexity and gradual elaboration of this belief system. Each human individual was considered to comprise not only a physical body but also three other crucial elements, known as the *ka*, *ba*, and *akh*, all of which were regarded as essential to human survival both before and after death. The name and shadow were also living entities, crucial to human existence, rather than simply linguistic and natural phenomena. The essence of each individual was contained in the sum of all these parts, none of which could be neglected.

This consciousness of individuals as composites of various types of identity brings us back again to the theme of dismemberment (and reassembling), which was discussed above with regard to the cult of Osiris. One of the reasons that such themes feature so prominently in Egyptian attitudes to death is because the act of ensuring any individual's enjoyment of the afterlife was a delicate business of separation and assembly. All of these separate elements (the body, *ka*, *ba*, *akh*, shadow, and name) had to be sustained and protected from harm. At the most basic level this could be achieved by burying the body with a set of funerary equipment, and in its most elaborate form the royal cult could include a number of temples complete with priests and a steady flow of offerings, usually financed by gifts of agricultural land and other economic resources. A wide diversity of surviving funerary texts (the Pyramid Texts, Coffin Texts, and various Books of the Netherworld) present an often conflicting set of descriptions of the afterlife, ranging from the transformation of humans into circumpolar stars to the continuation of normal life in an afterworld sometimes described as the Field of Reeds.

Ancient, modern, and postmodern mummies

Until recently it was assumed that the earliest *artificial* mummies (as opposed to bodies simply desiccated by the surrounding sand) were those found at cemeteries such as Abydos, Saqqara and Tarkhan in the Early Dynastic period, but in 1997 an Anglo-American team of archaeologists working in one of the non-elite Predynastic cemeteries at Hierakonpolis found three intact burials containing female bodies with their heads, necks and hands wrapped in linen bandages, the whole of each of the corpses being swathed in linen and matting. The grave goods accompanying these bodies dated to around 3600 BC (the early Naqada II culture), therefore pushing back the earliest use of artificial mummification to a much earlier period than previously supposed, although opinions differ as to whether the simple bandaging of parts of a corpse can necessarily be described as mummification. Intriguingly, one of the women had her throat cut after death, suggesting that even at this date there might have been a sense in which the ritual dismemberment and reassembly of Osiris's body-parts was being acted out. This is not the end of the story, however – the work of an Australian Egyptologist, Jana Jones, has demonstrated that the use of mummification techniques can probably be pushed back even further in time to the Badarian culture (c.4500–4100). Her examination of thick, desiccated clumps of wrappings from the Neolithic cemeteries at Badari and Mostagedda has shown that resin-soaked bandages were already being applied to bodies in a similar way to the Hierakonpolis examples. We therefore now have evidence for at least a thousand years of experimentation in mummification before the 1st Dynasty, although, as Jones points out,

> Whether the act of wrapping the body in the very earliest periods indicates an intention to preserve it artificially, or whether it was another aspect of the funerary ritual, is uncertain.

The practice of Egyptian mummification seems to have evolved simply to preserve the image of the body – thus some of the early mummies of the 3rd millennium BC were simply painted with plaster and paint, preserving the outer shell of the body but allowing the rest to decay away inside. The development of more sophisticated techniques meant that gradually more of the original body was retained, eventually reaching something of a peak in the late New Kingdom and Third Intermediate Period (c.1200–900 BC). By the time Herodotus wrote his detailed description of the process of mummification, around the middle of the 5th century BC, techniques are thought to have already gone into something of a decline, presumably partly in order to meet the demands of 'mass production' as mummification spread through larger numbers of the population.

The preservation of the body by mummification was an essential part of ancient Egyptian funerary practice, since it was to the body that the *ka*, or double, would return in order to find sustenance. If the body had disintegrated or become unrecognizable the *ka* would not be able to feed and the chances of reaching the afterlife would diminish.

My own first encounter with the concept of the Egyptian *ka* came in the form of a Dennis Wheatley novel: *The Ka of Gifford Hillary*, published in 1956, which must have played a small part in enticing me towards Egyptology. I now know that the eponymous ghost-like phenomenon in the novel (who manages to float around solving his own murder, like the central character in the 1980s movie *Ghost*) is probably more of a *ba* than a *ka* (see the glossary for the differences between the two), but considering the many much greater crimes committed against Egyptology by modern books and films, it seems a little churlish to pick on Dennis Wheatley, who had at least done a little research. Carter Lupton, Curator of Ancient History at the Milwaukee Public Museum, points out that 'Much of the lay person's "familiarity" with Egypt derives from popular fiction and film, which are often at odds with standard Egyptological interpretations.' Certainly to say that *The Mummy* (1998) was 'researched' would be to seriously strain the definition of the word.

Mummies (and their revival) have a very long literary and cinematic history, stretching back at least as far as 1827, when Jane Webb Loudon published *The Mummy – A Tale of the 22nd Century*, in which the mummy of Cheops, builder of the Great Pyramid, is resurrected. This book essentially belonged to the same genre as Mary Shelley's slightly earlier *Frankenstein*. Later novelists whose fiction pioneered the whole mummy genre include many whose names we would expect: Théophile Gautier (*The Mummy's Foot*, 1840), Edgar Allen Poe (*Some Words with a Mummy*, 1845), H. H. Rider Haggard (*She*, 1887; *Smith and the Pharaohs*, 1912–13), Sir Arthur Conan Doyle (*The Ring of Thoth*, 1890; *Lot No. 249*, 1892), Bram Stoker (*The Jewel of Seven Stars*, 1903), and Sax Rohmer (*She Who Sleeps*, 1928, and many others). One intriguing theory put forward by N. Daly is that the spate of late Victorian and Edwardian mummy tales was inspired by the changing nature of the British Empire, with the mummies subconsciously representing the dangerous and exotic materials pursued by empire-builders.

The first cinematic rendition of a resuscitated and vengeful mummy seems to have been *Cleopatra*, a one-minute-long silent movie made by George Melies, but the best-known feature-length film of this type is undoubtedly *The Mummy*, made in 1932 and starring Boris Karloff as Imhotep. The body of Imhotep is revived by archaeologists reading from a 'scroll of Thoth', a plot which actually draws on a rare example of an ancient Egyptian tale of a revived body, the cycle of Setne Khaemwaset, written in the demotic script in the Roman period. The principal literary source for this film seems to have been Nina Wilcox Putnam's *Cagliostro*, with Rider Haggard's *She* (the film version of which was written by John Balderston, who also wrote *The Mummy*) and Conan Doyle's *The Ring of Thoth* both also being possible influences. Since the 1930s, there have been numerous other mummy movies, in fact enough to have established this as very much a genre in its own right.

The curse . . .

In discussing mummies, we can hardly ignore the continual association in literature and films, particularly in the 20th century, between mummies and dreadful curses, usually affecting the archaeologist who has disturbed an Egyptian corpse's rest. Where did this all start, and more importantly is there any truth in it? One answer to the second part of the question is that, if these curses genuinely existed, then I and several of my Egyptological colleagues would surely have long ago succumbed to the kind of mosquito-infected cut that polished off Lord Carnarvon shortly after the opening of Tutankhamun's tomb. As for where it all started, there were certainly ancient Egyptian funerary inscriptions that included threats against those who might damage or neglect the tomb in some way, so there is very early evidence of a kind. However, if we want to find someone to blame for promoting the idea that such curses actually worked, then the name that springs immediately to mind is the Egyptologist Arthur Weigall, who was reporting as a journalist for the *Daily Mail* during the first few weeks of the removal of funerary equipment from Tutankhamun's tomb. As if the discovery in itself was not sufficiently exciting, Weigall seems to have hit upon the idea of mentioning the curse (although claiming not to believe in it himself) as a way of spicing up his dispatches. The first novelist to use the mummy's curse as part of a narrative was probably Louisa May Alcott, the writer of *Little Women*, who published a story called *Lost in a Pyramid; or the Mummy's Curse* in 1869, so Weigall would have been able to draw on a good 50 years of fictional material on this theme.

Chapter 8

Religion: Egyptian gods and temples

The pairs of cow's heads with huge curling horns depicted at the top of the Narmer Palette are part of the imagery of an early cow-goddess named Bat, who was patroness of the seventh nome (province) of Upper Egypt. She is a rather poorly known deity, partly because, by the Middle Kingdom, her cult had been absorbed into that of another much more prominent cow-goddess, Hathor. Unlike Hathor, who might be represented as a cow or cow-headed woman, Bat was portrayed (on the rare occasions that she appears in Egyptian art) with a body in the shape of the sistrum (a rattle-like musical instrument characteristically played by women). The body is not visible on the Narmer Palette, but Bat is described in the Pyramid Texts as 'with her two faces', which would tie in with her double representation on either side of the palette. Throughout the history of Egyptian religion the cults of minor deities were continually being absorbed into those whose cults were more widespread or more favoured by the kings of that time.

As Erik Hornung, one of the most influential researchers into Egyptian religion, has pointed out, 'In their constantly changing nature and manifestations, the Egyptian gods resemble the country's temples, which were never finished and complete, but always "under construction".' Hornung also argues that there was a probably a form of monotheism underlying the superficially polytheistic Egyptian religion for much of the pharaonic period. One argument is that the role of creator-god seems to have been one that transcended and subsumed numerous Egyptian gods, and another is that we need to take a relativistic viewpoint on religions:

> The world of the many gods is past; no one will ever again offer a bull to Amun or Zeus. But the present world of the sole God need not be the final one. Both correspond to stages of human consciousness, so that the categories of true or false are not applicable to them.

The cow's heads of Bat are an appropriate starting point for a consideration of Egyptologists' views on ancient Egyptian religion, given that images of hybrid animal-headed or bird-headed deities are usually the first ones that come to mind. It is noticeable also that these elaborate deities made up of human and bestial body-parts appear to interact directly with at least some of the human population of Egypt. Bruce Trigger has pointed out, in his book *Early Civilizations: Ancient Egypt in Context*, that one of the most important differences between our world-view and that of the Egyptians is that we make a clear distinction between the natural and supernatural worlds (as part of our inheritance of Greek philosophical thought) whereas the Egyptians saw both deities and humans as interacting on the same social and physical planes.

If ancient Egyptian culture as a whole is often difficult to comprehend, then Egyptian religion is among the most difficult of the topics that Egyptologists have tackled. A great deal of surviving Egyptian art is connected with religion, but usually it is much easier to describe and to categorize than to analyse or interpret effectively.

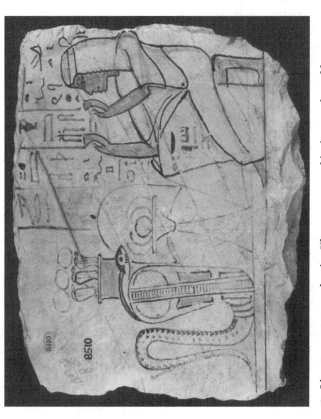

17. **Limestone ostracon, showing Khnummose worshipping a snake-goddess 19th Dynasty, c.1200 BC.**

Among the many questions that Egyptologists have had difficulties in answering effectively are the following. Did Egyptians actually imagine their deities to exist in the 'real world' as hybrids of human and non-human characteristics, from the surprisingly plausibly rendition of the god Horus as a falcon-headed man to the rather less convincing (to our eyes) representation of the sun-god Khepri as a man whose head is entirely substituted by a scarab beetle? Or did they simply create these images as elaborate symbols and metaphors representing the characteristics or personalities of their deities? When we are shown a jackal-headed figure embalming the body of the deceased are we supposed to believe that Anubis, the god of the underworld, was actually responsible for all mummifications or are we being shown a priest-embalmer wearing a mask allowing him to impersonate the god (and if so was he then regarded as actually becoming the god or simply imitating him during the ritual)? There is one surviving full-size pottery mask in the form of Anubis's jackal head (now in the Pelizaeus Museum, Hildesheim) but this does not really solve the above series of problems. Part of the urgency with which Egyptologists tend to attack such questions probably derives from our desire to find out whether the systems of thought of ancient Egypt were fundamentally different to our own, or whether they just appear so because they are expressed in ways that are now very difficult to interpret.

When most scholars write about Egyptian religion they focus principally on the archaeological remains of what appear to be sacred structures, and on the textual and iconographic clues to theological thought. Barry Kemp makes the point that most of our knowledge of Egyptian 'temple religion' is concerned with the symbolism and ritual of the large state temples, whereas we still know relatively little about the ways in which such buildings were used by people, whether priests, scribes, or normal members of the population. The masses were evidently rarely allowed to penetrate beyond the temples' outer courtyards, relying on festivals, when deities' images were sometimes carried from one shrine to another,

18. Predynastic female figurine with upraised arms, perhaps depicting an early goddess, c.3500 BC.

for the rare moments when they were able to gain any contact with the cult images. For many Egyptologists, this has led to the assertion that Egyptian religion was founded on the concepts of secrecy and revelation, both of which were bolstered and elaborated through myth, ritual, and temple architecture. It was in the course of rituals, festivals, and dramas that the divine reality seems to have been constantly acted out or actualized. Ritual and regular celebration of festivals were ways of repeatedly reinforcing the links between myth and reality. Each temple was therefore not simply the 'home' of one or more deities but a set of rooms connected with the performance of rituals and festivals. In a sense the temples simply served as a means of channelling and recording the movements of offerings and divine images in and out of the various shrines.

Religious origins

The history of Egyptian religion was at one stage concerned principally with the beliefs and temples of the pharaonic period, but it has become increasingly clear that, as with the rest of Egyptian culture, there is a significant prehistory of Egyptian religion that needs to be documented and analysed before the later material can be properly understood. At the Neolithic site of Nabta Playa (in the Western Desert, c.100 km west of Abu Simbel), for instance, circular and linear arrangements of small standing stones were identified in 1992, indicating that monuments oriented to astronomical phenomena (the cardinal points and the summer solstice) were already being created as early as 4000 BC. Alongside one of these alignments were found two tumuli covering burials of long-horned bulls, and further cattle burials, surmounted by large stones, were discovered in one of the wadis leading into the Nabta Playa depression, all of which strongly suggests that some form of cow/bull cult already existed among the cattle-herding people of the Egyptian deserts in the early 4th millennium BC, evidently prefiguring both the emergence of such cow-goddesses as Bat and Hathor and the very strong associations between Egyptian kings and bulls. Comparisons between female figures in early prehistoric petroglyphs, Predynastic female figurines, and some of the religious motifs of the pharaonic period appear to show a high degree of continuity in the iconography, although it would be simplistic to assume that the use of similar icons or artistic themes is necessarily an indication of long-term connections in the underlying religious beliefs.

In 1985, archaeology provided one intriguing insight into the crucial phase of religious development towards the end of Egyptian prehistory. Excavations in a section of the Predynastic town at Hierakonpolis (Locality HK29A) revealed a large area interpreted as an early religious complex, probably incorporating a parabolic courtyard, a colossal divine image of some kind, a ceremonial gateway, and four large post-holes which may show the location of a monumental façade, all dating to Naqada II–III (*c*.3500–3000). As with the Nabta Playa remains, there were copious traces of animal sacrifices in association with this likely early temple complex. Acts of animal sacrifice and the piling up of offerings to the gods seem to have been crucial elements of the early religion of Egypt, and in later times it is the dominant feature of Egyptian acts of worship.

Many of the texts inscribed on the walls of Egyptian temples are connected with the listing of the nature and quantity of offerings delivered to the gods' shrines. The walls of the mortuary temple of Ramesses III, for instance, are decorated with 71 offerings, the largest surviving set of offering lists in any of the New Kingdom royal mortuary temples. The most frequent kind of offering was bread (indeed the hieroglyph meaning 'offering' was a depiction of a loaf on a tray), with lists of more than 5,500 loaves and 204 jars of beer being offered every day. The loaves were of several different types, the most common being round *pesen* and tapering cylindrical moulded *bit*. This is one of the rare occasions where a fruitful connection can be made between the textual and archaeological sides of Egyptology, since sherds from the cylindrical *bit* bread-moulds have been found in abundance at Medinet Habu and other religious sites; these *bit* loaves seem to have been more closely associated with religious festivals than standard forms of bread.

If the provision of offerings represents the 'acceptable' side of Egyptian religion for the modern Western observer, there is also another recurrent aspect of many of the religious cults that Egyptologists of the late 19th and early 20th century frequently preferred to ignore (or at least gloss over). This was the tendency towards 'phallocentrism', involving cults dedicated to very obviously ithyphallic gods (especially Min and Amun). Although Egyptian art shied away from depicting the sexual act, it had no such qualms about the depiction of the erect phallus, for the simple reason that, as Tom Hare has pointed out, 'a celebration of the phallus is one of the central iconic foci of Egyptian religion from predynastic days through the Roman occupation'. The three oldest colossal religious statues in Egyptian history, found by Petrie in the earliest strata of the temple of Min at Koptos (and now in the Ashmolean Museum, Oxford), were essentially large ithyphallic representations, probably of Min, dating no later than the time of Narmer. This celebration of the phallus appears to be directly related to the Egyptians' concerns with the creation (and sustaining) of the universe, in which the king was thought to play a significant role – which was no doubt one of the reasons why the Egyptian state would have been concerned to ensure that the ithyphallic figures continued to be important elements of many cults (as in the phallocentrism of the Osiris cult, already discussed in Chapter 7).

Egyptian religion and kingship

Such is the king's domination of the evidence for religion in the pharaonic period that some Egyptologists have suggested that virtually all Egyptian religious cults are in some sense also designed to focus attention on the royal person. This situation is probably best expressed by the one phrase that suffuses a great deal of Egyptian religious practice: the so-called 'offering formula'. This phrase occurs at the beginning of lists of types of offerings and

consists of the words *hetep di nesw* ('an offering that the king gives').
In other words, each individual's acts of worship and offering to
deities were circumscribed by his or her links to the king. The
falcon-god Horus is one of the most prominent images on the front
of the Narmer Palette, suggesting that the king, who was very much
identified with Horus, was already playing a central role in the
celebration of religious cults and worship in the 1st Dynasty.

It might also be argued that the overall purpose of the Narmer
Palette was to serve as a kind of elaborate reference to the king's role
in the act of providing the gods with offerings, which might consist
of anything from fruit to slaughtered enemies or prisoners of war.
There are a number of constantly repeated iconographic themes in
the palette's decoration: first, the king smiting a foreigner, second,
the siege and capture of settlements, third, the binding up of
prisoners and their execution, and fourth, the offering of the spoils
of war to the Egyptian gods. These acts can all be encompassed
within a very simple theme in which the role of the Egyptian king
was to fight battles on behalf of the gods and then bring back the
prisoners and booty to dedicate to the gods in their temples.

Religion and ideology

A crucial distinction needs to be made between the above
discussion of the emergence and development of cults, shrines, and
temples, and, on the other hand, the surviving records of Egyptian
ideology and codes of social behaviour. The owners of tomb-chapels
in the Old Kingdom seem to have already felt a need to assert
their moral right to the monument that was ensuring their
enjoyment of the afterlife. Each of them would therefore claim that
the tomb had been built on new ground, and that the builders had
been paid and so on. Gradually, however, these more pragmatic
down-to-earth statements were supplemented by moral assertions.
The accepted code of social behaviour and the distinction between
right and wrong during the pharaonic period both tend to be closely
intertwined with funerary beliefs and cultic requirements. Thus the

earliest indications of Egyptian philosophical and ethical ideas perhaps inevitably are to be found embedded in funerary texts. These at first took the form of various statements included along with the offering formula, particularly on the so-called 'false-door stele' and later as elements in texts conventionally described as the 'autobiographies' of individuals, such as those of Harkhuf (at Aswan) or Ankhtifi (at Moalla), in which the deceased listed his or her good works. Ankhtifi, one of the few individuals whose life-story has survived from the First Intermediate Period, says:

> I am an honest man who has no equal, a man who can talk freely when others are obliged to be silent . . . The whole of Upper Egypt died from hunger and each individual had reached such a state of hunger that he ate his own children. But I refused to see anyone die of hunger in this province. I arranged for grain to be loaned to Upper Egypt and gave to the north grain from Upper Egypt. And I do not think that anything like this has been done by the provincial governors who came before me . . .

Ankhtifi is undoubtedly keen to establish links between his achievements as a local ruler and his moral authority. These funerary texts tend to be primarily concerned with justifying and vindicating the acts of individuals within an ethical context.

A number of practical statements of Egyptian ethics have survived in the form of the *sebayt* ('teachings'), which were mainly written on papyrus and date from the Old Kingdom to the Roman period (*c.*2500 BC–AD 325). The earliest of these documents describe the qualities required of a man in order to ensure success both in his lifetime and in the afterlife. Individuals were expected to satisfy their superiors and to protect those who were poorer. The earliest surviving *sebayt* (a series of maxims on the 'way of living truly') is the text said to have been composed by the 4th-Dynasty sage, Hardjedef (*c.*2525 BC), while another such document was attributed to Ptahhotep, a vizier of the 5th-Dynasty ruler Djedkara Isesi. It is likely that few of these instructions were written by their purported authors, and many, including that of Hardjedef, were almost certainly composed much later than they claim. The instructions retained their popularity throughout the pharaonic period, two of them being attributed to kings. The first of these was the *Instruction for King Merikara*, set in the First Intermediate Period (2181–2055), and the second was the *Instructions of Amenemhat I*, set at the beginning of the 12th Dynasty (*c.*1950).

From the 2nd millennium BC onwards, however, the code of ethics described in the *sebayt* was less worldly, tending to measure virtue more through piety to the gods than through material success. The two most important surviving instructions from the Greco-Roman period are the *Sayings of Ankhsheshonqy* (BM EA 10508) and the maxims recorded on Papyrus Insinger (Rijksmuseum, Leiden), which were both written in the demotic script, consisting of much shorter aphorisms compared with the *sebayt* of the pharaonic period.

Central both to Egyptian ethics and to their religious thought was the concept of Maat (often translated as 'truth' or 'harmony'), which harked back to the original state of tranquillity at the moment of the creation of the universe. When Erik Hornung was justifying the need for a study of ancient Egyptian patterns of thought and ideas (in his book *Idea into Image*) he argued that Egyptian religion was among the first attempts to answer universal questions:

> Along with the Sumerians, the Egyptians deliver our earliest – though by no means primitive – evidence of human thought . . . As far back as the third millennium B.C., the Egyptians were concerned with questions that return in later European philosophy and that remain unanswered even today – questions about being and nonbeing, about the meaning of death, about the nature of cosmos and man, about the essence of time, about the basis of human society and the legitimation of power.

Chapter 9

Egyptomania: the recycling and reinventing of Egypt's icons and images

The Narmer Palette was initially interpreted as a historical document recording a number of military successes over Libyans or Lower Egyptians by means of which the first unification of the Egyptian state was achieved (see Chapter 3). More recently, however, it has been suggested that the relief decoration simply depicts a number of rituals (probably relating to the kingship) enacted in the year that this palette was brought as an offering to the temple. Egyptologists have interpreted many other aspects of the Narmer Palette (as well as others made at around the same time) in a variety of ways. It therefore provides a useful indication of how Egyptologists analyse and interpret their raw data, often producing images of the past that subconsciously reflect their own contemporary social or political context.

Modern Egyptology is undoubtedly proliferating as a subject, effortlessly insinuating itself into all sorts of cultural areas where we might not previously have expected to find it, from contemporary art and music to Rosicrucianism, cigarette advertising and 'black awareness' groups. What was once the province of archaeologists, linguists, and slightly esoteric Afrocentrists such as Diop and Bernal has now become a much more pervasive mainstream product, with one recent hip-hop CD including 'Cleopatra and the tomb of Nefertiti' in a kind of shopping-list of items of black cultural heritage (I will deal later with the unfortunate but undeniable whiteness of Nefertiti, and probably also of the Greek Cleopatra for that matter).

Egyptology, or at least ancient Egypt itself, is heading rapidly in numerous different directions, and it is currently impossible to predict which of these will ultimately be the more fruitful, exciting, or problematic. One thing that can hardly be ignored, however, is the fact that Egypt is no longer simply the relatively obscure object of academic research – it is very much out there in the public domain, and there are any number of 'alternative Egypts' which, for better or worse, sit alongside what we might like to regard as the 'authentic' original. The players in this process of reinventing Egypt for different audiences and purposes range from journalists and artists to film producers, musicians, advertising executives, 'pyramidiots', and even, occasionally, university lecturers and museum curators. In this recycling and exploitation of the ancient Egyptian database, some aspects of the culture and history have tended to appeal more to different ages or audiences. Consequently, the modern non-Egyptological view of ancient Egypt is a dense patchwork built up of penny-dreadful mummy mysteries, Hollywood epics, New Age pseudo-scientific blockbusters, tacky tourist souvenirs, and also a few enduring icons – human faces and artefacts that have been plucked out of their original ancient context and left to float in a postmodern vacuum, at the whim of the observer. In this final chapter, I would like to examine the phenomenon of Egyptomania, whereby the flotsam and jetsam of ancient Egypt have somehow been washed up in the early 21st century, ending up in unexpected heaps scattered across our modern cultural landscape.

Interpretation in Egyptology: the case of pyramidology

One of the most obvious topics of fierce interpretative debate over the years has been the question of why the pyramids took the form that they did, and what this suggests about the purpose that they served. This 'pyramidology' is virtually a subject in its own right. Attention has focused not only on the shape but also on the precise size and spatial disposition of pyramids, as well as the detailed internal arrangement of the chambers. It almost goes without saying that many of the theories advanced have been among the least plausible or logical in the history of Egyptology, owing to the well-known effect that pyramids seem to exert on the mental faculties of some researchers. Not surprisingly, the choice of explanations at different points in time can tell us as much about the researchers as the problem.

A useful starting point is the very commonsensical explanation that the pyramidal shape is the most structurally sound way of building as high a monument as possible, with the most efficient use of building resources and greatest likelihood of long-term stability. For many people this has the disadvantage of ignoring the possibility of both (*a*) the colonization of earth by aliens from outer space and (*b*) a previously unsuspected civilization that already flourished thousands of years before the conventional emergence of ancient Egypt. It was also once seriously suggested to me that the pyramids had not been built but that they had been created by quarrying away all the surrounding stone – this doesn't actually explain their shape, but is a good example of the apparently inexhaustible thirst for explanations of pyramids that are imaginative rather than logical.

19. Professor Edouard Naville directing excavations at Tell Basta in 1886, in search of Biblical evidence.

A very long-lasting myth about the pyramids connects them with the biblical story of Joseph – as early as the 5th century AD, the Roman writer Julius Honorius suggested that they were Joseph's granaries. In 1859 John Taylor put forward the theory that the Great Pyramid was built by non-Egyptian invaders acting under God's guidance. Arab writers in the Middle Ages had a theory that the Pyramids were built at the time of Noah's flood in order to act as repositories of all the Egyptians' wisdom and scientific knowledge. The one thing that all of these suggestions have in common is their assumption that the pyramids were in some way linked with the role played by Egypt in the Bible, since many of the early scholars studying Egypt were theologically motivated. By the late 19th century many archaeological expeditions to Egypt had switched from treasure-hunting to the authentication of episodes in the Bible. The Society for the Promotion of Excavation in the Delta of the Nile (an early name for the British enthusiasts and academics who were eventually to form the Egypt Exploration Fund) was explicitly dedicated to the search for 'the documents of a lost period of Biblical history' in the Delta region, and it was for this reason that the sites initially excavated by Flinders Petrie and Edward Naville, on behalf of the Egypt Exploration Fund, included the Delta cities of Tanis, Bubastis Naukratis, Nabesha, and Defenna. This biblical concentration on Delta sites has had an unexpected benefit from the point of view of modern Egyptology in that many of these sites have deteriorated more severely than those further to the south, so 19th-century archaeologists' obsession with biblical connections now gives us some idea of the monuments at ancient cities that have virtually disappeared through 20th-century agricultural and urban expansion in the Delta.

To return to the pyramid debate, among the more recent discussions of pyramid form and purpose are those that emphasize the undoubted astronomical links of the pyramids. It has long been suggested that the so-called 'air vents' in the Great Pyramid served some astronomical function, since they are evidently carefully aligned with various stars, including the constellation of Orion (the

Egyptian god Sah), which might have been the intended destination of the king's *ba*, when he ascended to take his place among the circumpolar stars. More recently, Kate Spence, an Egyptologist at the University of Cambridge, has suggested that the architects of the pyramids must have aligned their sides with the cardinal points by sighting on two stars rotating around the position of the north pole (b-Ursae Minoris and z-Ursae Majoris). She points out that these stars would have been in perfect alignment at around 2467 BC, the precise date when Khufu's pyramid (the Great Pyramid) is thought to have been constructed. Her hypothesis is supported by the fact that inaccuracies in the orientations of earlier and later pyramids can be closely correlated with the degree to which the alignment of the two aforementioned stars deviates from true north.

Several well-publicized books have focused particularly on the so-called 'Orion Mystery', which is the suggestion that the layout of the three pyramids at Giza was intended to symbolize the pattern of the three stars making up the belt of Orion at around 10,500 BC. The tendency of such books to focus on the undoubted astronomical elements in pyramid design allows the writers to introduce speculation concerning the possible involvement of extra-terrestrial beings in pyramid construction (which can conveniently tap into modern popular cultural ideas such as those presented in the 1995 film *Stargate*). Although only a few writers since Eric von Daniken have gone so far as to suggest in print that aliens may have built certain monuments, the exploitation of astronomical aspects of the pyramids by researchers such as Robert Bauval and Graham Hancock allows them to at least imply some kind of 'outside' intervention.

The great Victorian enthusiast, Charles Piazzi Smyth, Astronomer Royal of Scotland and Professor of Astronomy at Edinburgh University, managed to combine both biblical and astronomical approaches in his pyramid research. Heavily influenced by the theories of the aforementioned John Taylor (who argued that the measurements of the pyramid amounted to a kind of slide-rule record of the proportions of the world as a whole), Piazzi Smyth surveyed at Giza in 1865 and declared that the Great Pyramid had been built at just the correct size in 'pyramid inches' to exactly encapsulate the circumference of earth, which, according to Taylor, the Egyptians were able to calculate through their knowledge of π. Piazzi Smyth then argued, in his three-volume *Life and Work at the Great Pyramid* (published in 1867), that the pyramid inch was also the unit of measurement used by the builders of Noah's Ark and Moses' tabernacle. Since the pyramid inch was conveniently virtually the same as the British inch, it was only a small step further to suggest that all this identified the British as the lost tribe of Israel, which neatly adds rampant Victorian imperialism to Piazzi Smyth's bundle of influences in his ruminations on pyramids.

Most Egyptologists argue that the real reasons for the physical form that the pyramids take must lie within the sphere of the Egyptians' own religious and funerary beliefs, as expressed in their texts and visual imagery. One possibility is that both the step-pyramid form and the true pyramid represent the primitive mound of sand, piled up over the earliest pit graves, perhaps also associated with the primeval mound of creation. Certain passages in the Pyramid Texts (inscribed on interior walls of pyramids from the late 5th Dynasty onwards) support the interpretation of the step pyramid (the earlier style, best exemplified by the 3rd-Dynasty pyramid of King Djoser at Saqqara) literally as a stairway up which the king could ascend to take his place among the stars. Elsewhere, the Pyramid Texts mention the king treading the rays of the sun in order to reach heaven, and the true pyramid might possibly therefore symbolize the rays of the sun fanning down to earth.

The above suggestions all fall within the familiar rationalist pattern, whereby Egyptologists use ancient data to explore the ways in which the ancient Egyptians themselves appear to be discussing the pyramids. Barry Kemp has summarized the way in which Egyptologists tend to use their knowledge – perhaps more 'creatively' than they are aware – when they attempt to reconstruct ancient Egyptian patterns of thought about such cultural phenomena as the pyramids:

> We can rethink ancient logic. But it creates an interesting pitfall, in that it is hard to know when to stop ... We really have no way of knowing in the end if a set of scholarly guesses which might be quite true to the spirit of ancient thought and well informed of the available sources ever actually passed through the minds of the ancients at all. Modern books and scholarly articles on ancient Egyptian religion are probably adding to the original body of thought as much as explaining it in modern western terms.

The Czech archaeologist Miroslav Verner comments on the pyramidological problem:

> People are always going to dream, and therefore there will always be some who want to delve into certain mysteries and others who throw themselves into the adventure of scientific enquiry. They will always be moving along the path, but they will never meet each other.

Amarna issues

It is probably some kind of record (and perverse in the extreme) to have come this close to the end of a general book on Egyptology without having provided any detailed discussion of Akhenaten, Nefertiti, or Cleopatra – clearly among the most popular icons of ancient Egypt (the fourth member of this select group being of course Tutankhamun). These ancient individuals, apart from being the most fascinating aspects of the subject for many modern enthusiasts, have been foremost in the transformation of Egyptology into a vibrant part of 21st-century popular culture. The ways in which these icons have been exploited can therefore give a general sense of the absorption of Egypt into the mass media.

In obedience to chronological order, we should deal with Akhenaten and Nefertiti first. Undoubtedly, Akhenaten's reign, in the mid-14th century BC, was the most unusual religious and artistic phase of the Egyptian New Kingdom (1550–1069), if not the entire pharaonic period. During the first few years of his reign he appears to have developed an obsession with the cult of the Aten (literally the 'sun-disc'), a considerably more abstract deity than the traditional Egyptian pantheon. He built religious monuments to the Aten at a number of sites, but primarily at eastern Karnak and at Akhetaten ('horizon of the Aten'), the latter being a new capital city established by him on supposedly virgin ground at the site now known as Amarna in Middle Egypt. It is Amarna that has given its name to the period encompassing the reigns of Akhenaten and his brief successors. Because Akhenaten and his activities were reviled soon after his death, virtually all of his monuments were dismantled and his name was erased from those that remained. Consequently, it was not until the work of 19th-century archaeologists that the history of the Amarna period began to be reconstructed from the many surviving fragments. As Erik Hornung puts it,

Egyptomania

> Akhenaten himself, forgotten for so long, now appears before us as one of the great founders of religion, and the first one whom we can grasp. 'Hero' or 'Heretic' – he definitely belongs not just to Ancient Egypt, but to human history.

It is interesting to trace views of Akhenaten from the early 20th century onwards. Initially his stock is high, and Arthur Weigall's 'biography' of the king paints him as the founder of a 'religion so pure that one must compare it with Christianity to discover its faults', while Thomas Mann makes him the hero of his romantic novel *Joseph*, but by the 1950s Eberhard Otto was describing him as egocentric, ugly, and despotic, and in the 1980s Donald Redford argued that 'Akhenaten destroyed much, he created little . . . Akhenaten, whatever else he may have been, was no intellectual heavyweight'.

The high profile of Akhenaten in modern times is not so much because of any particularly detailed awareness of the architecture of his temples or his iconoclastic religious ideas (although these have had a significant impact on some more recent faiths and philosophies, such as Rosicrucianism), but because of the very striking and unusual appearance of much of the *art* of his reign. The king himself is shown as a long-faced, bulbous-chinned, thick-lipped, and fat-bellied figure, apparently with female breasts and swollen thighs, rather than being idealized as a youthful paragon of manhood as was usually the case with Egyptian kings (and according to the chief royal sculptor Bak, it was the king himself who had authorized this style of art). As in other periods, both the royal family and the elite officials surrounding the king were depicted in a similar way, thus ensuring that all those Amarna-period works of art that include human figures are fairly easy to recognize. This has also led to the production of a large number of fakes and forgeries of Amarna sculptures, since the exaggerated style is relatively easy to copy (and also very popular with the buyers of antiquities). In the case of the Mansoor private collection of antiquities, a very large group of Amarna pieces have been subject to intense dispute concerning their authenticity. There is also said to have been a stronger sense of freedom and creativity in Amarna art, although this perception is no doubt partly the result of the changes in religious subject matter and the survival of an unusual number of paintings from within houses and palaces as opposed to temples and tombs.

It is not clear whether the artistic distortions of Amarna 'portraits' constitute a realistic record of Akhenaten's appearance (which would imply that he suffered from some form of disease) or whether there is a more symbolic reason for his androgynous appearance, perhaps relating to an attempt to personify both male and female aspects of fecundity. Some Egyptologists have suggested, for instance, that the bisexual appearance of the Amarna-style human figures might echo the form of Hapy, the god of the Nile inundation, whose body was deliberately intended to convey the idea of both male and female fertility.

The first full-blown attempt to explain Akhenaten's appearance medically was the proposal by the ubiquitous Sir Grafton Elliot Smith that the king may have suffered from Froehlich's Syndrome, an endocrine disorder which can have similar effects on the body. The disadvantage of this solution is that sufferers from this syndrome are also usually not only mentally retarded but incapable of producing children, neither of which could be applied to Akhenaten, with at least six girls by Nefertiti (and two other girls who seem to have resulted from incestuous relationships between the king and his own daughters). An alternative suggestion, first put forward by the Canadian Alwyn Burridge, is that Akhenaten might instead have suffered from Marfan's Syndrome. Quite a good case can be made for the latter (which is a severe disorder caused by a single abnormal gene), given that the symptoms include a pigeon chest, a wide pelvic area, elongated skull, spidery fingers and a long face with protruding chin, and it would be additionally applicable given that sufferers and their children were susceptible to sudden death (through weakness of the cardiovascular system). Symptoms also include likely blindness, which might possibly tie in with his obsession with the sun-disc, given that it may have been the only phenomenon that he could perceive. There are still, however, many Egyptologists who argue that such physical and medical theories take the appearance of the art far too literally, and that the peculiarities of the representations of the Amarna royal family might have lain much more within the realm of symbol and metaphor. The likelihood that we are dealing with a chosen style rather than a physical condition is backed up by surviving depictions of Akhenaten in the early part of his reign (before he had fully espoused Atenism and changed his name from Amenhotep), which show him with the standard idealized features more reminiscent of his father.

All of the above factors have the effect of making Akhenaten, his wife Nefertiti, and the Amarna period over which they presided endlessly fascinating to the modern observer. There are any number of 'mysteries' about the period, and constant opportunities for speculation on such topics as why Nefertiti disappears from the records before the end of Akhenaten's reign, or whether she perhaps reinvented herself as the the ostensibly male ruler Smenkhkare, who enjoyed a very brief period of joint rule with Akhenaten at the end of the Amarna period. One of the other burning questions concerns the fate of the corpses of the entire Amarna family: where were they initially buried and where are they now? Then there are the barrage of questions about Akhenaten's ideology and personality: was he a saintly monotheist who anticipated (or even precipitated) the rise of the Jewish faith, or was he an unreasonable tyrant who almost ran the Egyptian economy into the ground (or all of the above at the same time!)?

It was not until the late 19th century that Egyptologists became fully aware of Akhenaten and the Amarna period but, as John Ray has pointed out, in a somewhat tongue-in-cheek assessment, the timing of Akhenaten's emergence from the shadows could not have been better:

> the 20th century turned out to be made for him: he could be seen as a tortured genius who took on a sclerotic establishment, a loving husband and father, an exceptional visionary and artist, a pacifist who believed in human brotherhood and a master of religious symbolism.

One of the tantalizing aspects of the Amarna period is that we have an enormous quantity of artistic, monumental, and textual data, and yet we still do not seem to have enough evidence to reconstruct anything like the full picture of this remarkable but relatively brief phase in Egyptian history. As the British Egyptologist Nicholas Reeves has put it, 'the real problem with Amarna is not so much a shortage of good evidence as a superabundance of speculation misrepresented as fact'.

Given Reeves's statement, it is perhaps appropriate that there have been numerous fictional rewritings of the Amarna episode, including a Noel-Coward style play by Agatha Christie (*Akhnaten*) in which one of the characters says, 'Akhenaten and I would never have got on. I don't believe he's got any sense of humour. He's so frightfully religious too.' There has been an Amarna opera: first performed in 1984, Philip Glass's *Akhnaten* used his non-Western-influenced minimalist musical style, together with a libretto including ancient Egyptian, Akkadian, and Hebrew, to conjure up a poignant picture of Akhenaten and Nefertiti as tragic figures, whose spirits eventually haunt the ruins of their abandoned city at Amarna. We can add to this one of the most famous Hollywood forays into ancient Egypt with *The Egyptian*, directed by Michael Curtiz in 1954; based on Mika Waltari's novel, it is set in Akhenaten's court and starred Victor Mature as Horemheb. Each of these renditions of Amarna is as idiosyncratic as the last, and the one thing they have in common is their tendency to cast Akhenaten as a revolutionary dreamer and visionary.

Perhaps the most sensible thing that anyone has said about the Amarna period is Margaret Murray's comment in 1949 (ironically even before the Akhenaten-industry had fully built up steam) that

> The Tell el-Amarna period has had more nonsense written about it than any other period in Egyptian history ... In the case of Akhenaten, the facts do not bear the construction often put on them.

Icons and sirens: Egyptian femmes fatales

As if all the above were not enough, the Amarna period has yielded one particular artistic icon that somehow manages to combine the sexual attraction of Marilyn Monroe with the deadly controversy of the Elgin Marbles, and perhaps a little added spice of racism and fascism. This is of course the bust of Nefertiti.

20. The bust of Queen Nefertiti, c.1350 BC.

The German excavator Ludwig Borchardt discovered the famous painted limestone bust of Nefertiti in 1912, in the workshop of the sculptor Thutmose, whose house was one of the large sprawling villas in the southern part of the city at Amarna. The sculpture – probably intended as a sculptor's model rather than a finished piece in itself – is about 50 cm high and fantastically well preserved, its only flaw being the absence of the right eye (although remarkably this does not particularly impair its overall beauty). The circumstances by which the bust ended up in the Berlin museum, however, have been a source of heated debate ever since. According to Nicholas Reeves,

> At the formal division of spoils a mere month after the discovery, the Nefertiti bust passed to Dr James Simon, the sponsor of the German excavations. In 1920 Simon made a formal gift of his collection to the state of Prussia; three years after that, the queen was unveiled to an astonished public – an event closely followed by outraged complaints from the Egyptian Government that the queen's portrait had left Egypt under irregular circumstances. Accusations flew and solutions were proposed in an attempt to resolve this unhappy situation – but to no avail . . .

If the bust arrived in Europe amid controversy, the situation if anything became worse by the 1930s, when Adolf Hitler himself declared that it was his favourite work of art from Egypt, and would therefore remain in Germany.

The link with Hitler is perhaps no accident, since one of the other controversial aspects of the sculpture is the fact that it has such characteristically European, rather than African facial characteristics. This has meant that, for many Afrocentrists, it symbolizes traditional Egyptologists' supposed determination to present Egyptian culture as non-African and non-black. In the catalogue of the polemical exhibition 'Egypt in Africa' in 1996, Asa G. Hilliard III, Professor of Education at Georgia State University, argued,

This exhibit is one of the first to select items that show more typical African phenotypes rather than the atypical and sometimes foreign images that most Europeans like to see, e.g. Nefertiti, the Sheik el Bilad, or Kai the scribe, those ambiguous enough to be regarded as 'white'.

The bust seems to belong to the later part of the Amarna period, when the new artistic style had settled down, and become much less extreme. In the eyes of some observers it is the most aesthetically pleasing image of a woman's face ever produced. In an attempt to analyse why this should be the case, Jaromir Malek suggests that

> Much of the attraction of the piece stems from its perfect, almost geometrical, regularity which is so appealing to our modern eyes: long straight lines predominate, most conspicuously those connecting the front of the crown and the queen's forehead on profile, and the side of the crown and her cheeks on front view.

Even by the standards of 18th-Dynasty royal women, such as Ahhotep I and Hatshepsut, the real historical Nefertiti, principal wife of Akhenaten, seems to have achieved unusual power and influence, perhaps building on the achievements of her influential mother-in-law (and perhaps also aunt) Queen Tiye. Camille Paglia paints a lurid Lady-Macbeth-like portrait of Nefertiti:

> The proper response to the Nefertiti bust is fear. The queen is an android, a manufactured being. She is a new gorgoneion, a 'bodiless head of fright' ... Art shows Akhenaten half-feminine, his limbs shrunken and belly bulging, possibly from birth defect or disease. This portrait shows his queen half-masculine, a vampire of political will.

Whether we agree with Paglia's characteristically over-the-top description or not, it shows the continuing power of this bust – and by extension, Nefertiti herself – to evoke passionate responses.

There can be few sculptures that are so closely identified with the individual depicted that commentators discuss the bust as if it were in some sense the actual woman, which is after all a very characteristically ancient Egyptian position to take.

The way in which the statue itself is regarded almost as a sacred relic was demonstrated in 2003, when two artists ('Little Warsaw') effectively 'restored' the whole sculpture, creating a body to support the bust, as part of the Hungarian Pavilion at the Venice Biennale. In the end, the head was not allowed to travel to Venice to be displayed along with the body, but a curiously evocative photograph was taken, showing the old head and new body joined together and standing upright beside the empty display case in Berlin (as if Nefertiti had come through time to visit her own bust but found it missing). This was a powerful artistic image, but on a museological and Egyptological level it was considered inappropriate to treat the object in this cavalier way, and relations between the Berlin Egyptian Museum and the Supreme Council for Antiquities in Cairo were again somewhat soured – the original plan to display both head and body together in Venice was abandoned. In the booklet accompanying the display of *The Body of Nefertiti*, the artists point out that,

> It became evident that Nefertiti had been studied to death by Egyptologists: the only way to revive her seemed to be by replanting her into the context of contemporary art.

They also have something to say on the racial debate:

> This statue is one of the important sources of European cultural history and sculpture, even though it was created outside the continent. Its outsider position adds further meanings to the project of completing: this 3000 year old model of beauty has been contributing, ever since it was found and put on public display, to the European ideal of beauty, even though it is both culturally and historically non-European.

If this quotation suggests that Nefertiti has been exploited to some extent as a conveniently Europeanized image of Egypt, then it could be argued that something of the same sense of a bridge between Egypt and Europe can be found in the ways in which Cleopatra has been portrayed. Certainly Queen Cleopatra VII Thea Philopator, the most famous of the seven Cleopatras, long ago became such an icon and symbol of the decadent Orient that – cliché though it may be – the real woman has become increasingly difficult to find. In the immediate aftermath of the Battle of Actium and her suicide, Roman writers such as Horace and Propertius still regarded her primarily as the scheming and decadent figure who had destroyed the reputation of Mark Antony and threatened the stability of the Roman Empire, but once she was dead they could allow themselves a little more sympathy for her. In one of his odes, Horace calls her *fatale monstrum*, which can be translated literally as 'death-threatening monster', but can also have the more intriguing sense of 'miraculous one sent by destiny', conveying the growing sense that she was a fascinating and tragic figure in her own right, rather than simply a symbol of the slothful Orient.

Even without the filmic contributions of Claudette Colbert, Vivien Leigh, and Elizabeth Taylor, Cleopatra would probably be a close rival to Nefertiti in her popular reputation for beauty, but our real knowledge of her physical appearance is actually quite tenuous. Indeed in a speech in 1969, André Malraux commented that 'Nefertiti is a face without a queen, Cleopatra is a queen without a face.' It tends to be assumed that Cleopatra was largely Greek in appearance, on the basis of her Macedonian/Ptolemaic ancestry, and the fact that she is said to have learnt Egyptian certainly implies that she was probably both racially and culturally more Greek than Egyptian. Although Boccaccio described her as 'famous for nothing but her beauty', the portraits on contemporary coins show a woman who is distinctive rather than pretty, and Plutarch claims that 'her beauty was not in and for itself incomparable, nor such to strike the person who was just looking at her; but her conversation had an irresistible charm'.

21. Elizabeth Taylor as Cleopatra and Richard Burton as Mark Antony in a scene from *Antony and Cleopatra* (1963).

If sparkling conversation was actually the queen's best feature, it seems a shame that so few of her cinematic portrayals have had any humour in them. One of the few comedies to tackle the theme of Antony and Cleopatra was the British film *Carry on Cleo* (1964), which is perhaps best remembered for Amanda Barrie's unusually girl-next-door rendition of Cleopatra, and Kenneth Williams's entirely unique version of Julius Caesar ('Infamy, infamy, they've all got it in for me!').

In her cinematic incarnations Cleopatra was always played by white women, and indeed in Cecil B. DeMille's Cleopatra film one naïve character is ridiculed for asking whether Cleopatra is black. Nevertheless it is presumably because Cleopatra has become such a powerful symbol of Egypt in general that there have been attempts to claim not only that she was of pure Egyptian blood but that she was a black woman. Mary Hamer, author of a book on the myth of Cleopatra, comments:

> Today controversy rages again over the body of Cleopatra and, in particular, over her race. When black nationalists in the United States lay claim to Cleopatra, as they do, that attempt is surely made in the pursuit of a dignity and respect that have been denied to black families and their way of life. Countering them are mainly white scholars, who, in defence of 'civilisation' and 'scientific knowledge', as they put it, insist that Cleopatra could not have been black.

It is primarily through the cinema and theatre (e.g. Bernard Shaw's *Caesar and Cleopatra*) rather than archaeology that the reputation of Cleopatra has continued to flourish during the 20th and early 21st centuries. However, recent Franco-Egyptian excavations in the ancient harbour areas of Alexandria have revealed many submerged sculptures and fragments of architecture from the remains of Ptolemaic and Roman buildings now on the seabed. The fact that this work as a whole is popularly described (both by archaeologists and journalists) as the excavation of 'Cleopatra's palace' is not

surprising – Cleopatra is just too powerful a 'brand' to resist
(after all, both Nefertiti and Cleopatra are the names of Egyptian
cigarettes). Two of the sculptures retrieved by the French marine
archaeologists have been tentatively identified as Ceasarion,
Cleopatra's son by Julius Ceasar, and another is probably Ptolemy
XII, her father. It would be nice to think that somewhere on the sea
floor off Alexandria there is a dazzling bust of Cleopatra to compare
with the Nefertiti one in Berlin.

Too many 'alternative Egypts'?

In this discussion of the sculpting and deconstruction of the images
of Akhenaten, Nefertiti, and Cleopatra, I have concentrated
primarily on the way in which they have been transformed and
appropriated by artists, writers, and film-makers. Before I finish,
I also need to discuss the rise of the 'alternative' Egyptologist.
In the 1990s, as the Western world approached the end of its
2nd millennium AD, there was a general upsurge in 'New Age'
books and documentaries, some of which promoted maverick
and non-academic approaches to the archaeology and texts of
ancient Egypt. This was only the most recent flowering of a
phenomenon that stretched further back than Egyptology itself,
already encountered in the theories of such 19th-century writers as
John Taylor and Charles Piazzi Smyth.

Alternative Egyptologists generally use a pick'n'mix method,
selecting the data they want and ignoring or rejecting other
evidence that is less conducive to their arguments. This is because
they usually start with an answer rather than a problem or question,
then they search around for the data to prove it. Such an approach
is exactly the opposite of conventional 'problem-oriented'
archaeological research techniques in which the researcher starts
with a problem (e.g. what did Early Dynastic royal tombs look like?)
and then explores and assesses relevant data in order to try to find
one or more possible answers. The alternative researcher might be
characterized as 'answer-oriented' in that the conclusion of such a

book could easily be written before the data were assembled. One inevitable result of the pick'n'mix approach is that the alternative researchers occasionally use data that are well-known or well-accepted by traditional academics. In the case of the pyramids, for instance, the information concerning the alignment of certain 'air-shafts' in the Great Pyramid with astronomical phenomena had been published by the Egyptologist I. E. S. Edwards long before Bauval's best-selling *Orion Mystery* appeared. Similarly, the visual links between the sites of Heliopolis and Giza, taking the form of demonstrable sight-lines between the monuments, were studied and described by University College London lecturer, David Jeffreys, as well as forming part of Bauval's hypothesis.

Within the scope of this book, devoted mainly to the archaeology and history of ancient Egypt, I have only been able to dip my toe occasionally into the vast ocean of alternative approaches to Egypt, and the ways in which Egyptian ideas, motifs, and stories have been reworked and reappropriated by modern artists, architects, writers, musicians, and dramatists. The alternative Egypts, from Boris Karloff's resurrected mummy to Bernal's 'Black Athena' and Philip Glass's operatic *Akhenaten*, deserve several books all to themselves.

From 'wonderful things' to 'wonderful fellows'

The 'wonderful things' quote attributed to Howard Carter when asked by Lord Carnarvon what he could see when he first looked into the burial chamber of Tutankhamun is part of the high camp charm not only of ancient Egypt but also of Egyptology itself. Europeans and Americans wearing pith helmets, riding on camels, posing in their Edwardian best suits outside royal tombs, and dressing up in Ottoman finery are as much part of our modern mental view of Egypt as all the surviving ancient images.

One of the most popular versions of Egypt to have been conjured up by a modern writer is the louche cruise-boat world evoked by

Agatha Christie in her 1937 Poirot novel *Death on the Nile* (beautifully translated into the 1978 film of the same name), and what better way to end this Very Short Introduction than with a short piece of understatement from one of her characters, Simon Doyle:

> You know, I'm not much of a fellow for temples and sight-seeing and all that, but a place like this sort of gets you, if you know what I mean. Those old Pharaohs must have been wonderful fellows.

References

Chapter 1: Introduction

Bruce Trigger, 'The Narmer Palette in Cross-Cultural Perspective', in M. Görg and E. Pusch (eds), *Festschrift Elmar Edel* (Bamberg, 1979), p. 415

Barry Kemp, *Ancient Egypt: Anatomy of a Civilization* (London, 1989), p. 3

Tom Hare, *ReMembering Osiris* (Stanford, Calif., 1999), p. 4

Alan Lloyd, 'Herodotus', in K. Bard (ed.) *Encyclopedia of the Archaeology of Ancient Egypt* (London & New York, 1999), p. 371.

John Laughlin, *Archaeology and the Bible* (London, 2000), p. 90

Jan Assmann, *Moses the Egyptian* (Cambridge, Mass., 1997), p. 209

John Romer, *Testament: The Bible and History* (London, 1988), p. 71

John Wortham, *British Egyptology: 1549–1906* (Newton Abbot, 1971), p. 106

Bruce Trigger, *A History of Archaeological Thought* (Cambridge, 1989)

Chapter 2: Discovering and inventing

James Quibell and Frederick Green, *Hierakonpolis II* (London, 1902), p. 30

Michael Hoffman, *Egypt before the Pharaohs* (London, 1979), p. 129

Archibald Sayce, *The Archaeology of the Cuneiform Inscriptions*, 2nd edn. (London, 1908), p. 188

John Laughlin, *Archaeology and the Bible* (London, 2000), p. 85

Eric Peet, *The Present State of Egyptological Studies* (Oxford, 1934)

Chapter 3: History

Bruce Trigger, *A History of Archaeological Thought* (Cambridge, 1989), p. 154

Toby Wikinson, *Early Dynastic Egypt* (London, 1999), p. 44

Erik Hornung, *Idea into Image* (New York, 1992), pp. 147–66

Donald Redford, *Pharaonic King-lists, Annals and Day-Books: A Contribution to the Egyptian Sense of History* (Mississauga, 1986), p. xix

Barry Kemp, *Ancient Egypt: Anatomy of a Civilization* (London, 1989), p. 5

Stephan Seidlmayer, 'First Intermediate Period', in I. Shaw (ed.) *The Oxford History of Ancient Egypt* (Oxford, 2000), p. 120

Chapter 4: Writing

Walter Fairservis Jr, 'A Revised View of the Na'rmr Palette', *Journal of the American Research Center in Egypt*, 28 (1991), 1–20

Jean-Claude Gardin, *Archaeological Constructs: An Aspect of Theoretical Archaeology* (Cambridge, 1980), p. 3

Barry Kemp, 'Large Middle Kingdom Granary Buildings (and the Archaeology of Administration)', *Zeitschrift für Ägyptische Sprache und Altertumskunde*, 113 (1986), 120–36

David O'Connor, 'Political Systems and Archaeological Data in Egypt: 2600–1780 BC', *World Archaeology*, 6 (1974), 15–38

Chapter 5: Kingship

Alan Gardiner, *Egypt of the Pharaohs* (Oxford, 1961), pp. 184–98

Nicolas Grimal, *A History of Ancient Egypt*, tr. I. Shaw (Oxford, 1992), pp. 210–18

Peter der Manuelian, *Studies in the Reign of Amenophis II* (Hildesheim, 1987), p. 191

John Wilson, *The Burden of Egypt* (Chicago, 1951), pp. 174–5

Donald Redford, *History and Chronology of the Eighteenth Dynasty of Egypt* (Toronto, 1967), pp. 63–4, 85–6

Suzanne Ratié, *La Reine Hatchepsout: Sources et problèmes* (Leiden, 1979), p. 264

Michael Rice, *Egypt's Legacy* (London, 1997), p. 149

Grafton Elliot Smith, *The Royal Mummies* (Cairo, 1912), p. 59

Bruce Trigger, *A History of Archaeological Thought* (Cambridge, 1989), p. 153

Amelia Edwards, *A Thousand Miles up the Nile* (London, 1888), 282–3

Kenneth Kitchen, *Pharaoh Triumphant* (Warminster, 1982), p. 237

Jan Assmann, *The Search for God in Ancient Egypt* (Ithaca and London, 2001), p. 122

Chapter 6: Identity

Toby Wilkinson, 'What a King is This: Narmer and the Concept of the Ruler', *Journal of Egyptian Archaeology*, 86 (2000), 29

Cheikh Anta Diop, 'Origin of the Ancient Egyptians', in G. Mokhtar (ed.), *General History of Africa II* (Berkeley, Calif., 1981), p. 36

Cheikh Anta Diop, *Precolonial Black Africa* (New York, 1987), p. 217

Molefi Kete Asante, 'Early African Cultures: An Afrocentric Perspective', in Theodore Celenko (ed.) *Egypt in Africa* (Indianapolis, 1996), p. 33

C. Loring Brace *et al.*, in M. R. Lefkowitz and G. M. Roberts (eds), *Black Athena Revisited* (Chapel Hill and London, 1996), p. 162

Whitney Davis, *Masking the Blow* (Los Angeles, 1992), p. 165

Raymond Faulkner, *The Ancient Egyptian Pyramid Texts* (Oxford, 1969), p. 198

E. A. Wallis Budge, *The Gods of the Egyptians I* (London, 1904), p. 297

James Henry Breasted, *Development of Religion and Thought in Ancient Egypt* (New York, 1912), p. 11

Lynn Meskell, 'Desperately Seeking Gender: A Review Article', *Archaeological Review from Cambridge*, 13/1 (1994), 109.

Tom Hare, *ReMembering Osiris* (Stanford, Calif., 1999), pp. 139, 144

Chapter 7: Death

Jana Jones, 'Towards Mummification: New Evidence for Early Developments', *Egyptian Archaeology*, 21 (2002), 5–7

Carter Lupton, '"Mummymania" for the Masses – is Egyptology Cursed by the Mummy's Curse', *Consuming Ancient Egypt*, ed. S. MacDonald and M. Rice (London, 2003), pp. 23–46

Chapter 8: Religion

Erik Hornung, *Conceptions of God in Ancient Egypt: The One and The Many*, tr. J. Baines (London, 1982), pp. 255–6

Bruce Trigger, *Early Civilizations: Ancient Egypt in Context* (Cairo, 1993), pp. 87, 93

Barry Kemp, 'How Religious were the Ancient Egyptians?', *Cambridge Archaeological Journal*, 5/1 (1995), 26

Tom Hare, *ReMembering Osiris* (Stanford, Calif., 1999), p. 145

Ankhtifi's biography is quoted from Nicolas Grimal, *A History of Ancient Egypt* (Oxford, 1992), p. 142

Erik Hornung, *Idea into Image: Essays on Ancient Egyptian Thought* (Princeton, 1992), p. 13

Chapter 9: Egyptomania: the recycling and reinventing of Egypt's icons and images

Barry Kemp, *Ancient Egypt: Anatomy of a Civilization* (London, 1989), pp. 4–5

Miroslav Verner, *The Pyramids: Their Archaeology and History* (New York, 2001), p. 459

Erik Hornung, 'The Rediscovery of Akhenaten and his Place in Religion', *Journal of the American Research Center in Egypt*, 29 (1992), 49

Donald Redford, 'Monotheism of a Heretic', *Biblical Archaeology Review*, 13/3 (1987), 28

John Ray, 'Akhenaten: Hero or Heretic', *The Times* (London, 21 Mar. 2001)

Nicholas Reeves, *Akhenaten: Egypt's False Prophet* (London, 2001), p. 9

Margaret Murray, *The Splendour that was Egypt* (London, 1949), p. 54

Nicholas Reeves, *Ancient Egypt: The Great Discoveries* (London, 2000), p. 136

Asa G. Hilliard III, 'Are Africans African? Scholarship over Rhetoric and Propaganda. Valid Discourse on Kemetic Origins', in Theodore Celenko (ed.) *Egypt in Africa* (Indianapolis, 1996), p. 113

Jaromir Malek, *Egypt: 4000 years of Art* (London, 2003), p. 190

Camille Paglia, *Sexual Personae: Art and Decadence from Nefertiti to Emily Dickinson* (New York, 1991), pp. 68–9

Little Warsaw, *The Body of Nefertiti* (Budapest, 2003), pp. 4–6

Mary Hamer, 'The Myth of Clepatra since the Renaissance', in S. Walker and P. Higgs (eds), *Cleopatra of Egypt: from History to Myth* (London, 2001), p. 310

Agatha Christie, *Death on the Nile* (London, 1937), p. 80

Further reading

Preface

Numerous books and articles discuss the Narmer Palette and other Protodynastic palettes and mace-heads. A few of the more interesting ones are: James Quibell and Frederick Green, *Hierakonpolis*, 2 vols. (London, 1900–2); Elise J. Baumgartel, *The Cultures of Prehistoric Egypt II* (London, 1960); Bruce Trigger, 'The Narmer Palette in Cross-Cultural Perspective', in M. Görg and E. Pusch (eds), *Festschrift Elmar Edel* (Bamberg, 1979), pp. 409–19; Bruce Williams, 'Narmer and the Coptos Colossi', *Journal of the American Research Center in Egypt*, 25 (1988), 93–101; Nicholas Millett, 'The Narmer Macehead and Related Objects', *Journal of the American Research Center in Egypt*, 27 (1990), 53–9; Walter Fairservis, jun., 'A Revised View of the Na'rmr Palette', *Journal of the American Research Center in Egypt*, 28 (1991), 1–20; Whitney Davis, *Masking the Blow* (Berkeley, 1992); David Wengrow, 'Rethinking "Cattle Cults" in Early Egypt: Towards a Prehistoric Perspective on the Narmer Palette', *Cambridge Archaeological Journal*, 11/1 (2001), 91–104.

Chapter 1: Introduction

The following general reference works are well worth consulting: Barry Kemp, *Ancient Egypt: Anatomy of a Civilization* (London, 1989); Eugen Strouhal: *Life in Ancient Egypt* (Cambridge, 1992); Ian Shaw and Paul Nicholson, *The British Museum Dictionary of Ancient Egypt* (London, 1995); Serge Donadoni (ed.), *The Egyptians* (Chicago, 1997);

Regina Schulz and Matthias Seidel (eds), *Egypt: The World of the Pharaohs* (Cologne, 1998).

For Egypt and the Greeks see John Wilson, *Herodotus in Egypt* (Leiden, 1970); Alan Lloyd, *Herodotus Book II.1: An Introduction* (Leiden, 1975); A. K. Bowman, *Egypt after the Pharaohs* (London, 1986); Naphthali Lewis, *Greeks in Ptolemaic Egypt* (Oxford, 1986); Roger Matthews and Cornelia Roemer, *Ancient Perspectives on Egypt* (London, 2003).

For Egypt and the Bible, see Pierre Montet, *Egypt and the Bible* (Philadelphia, 1968); Donald Redford, *A Study of the Biblical Story of Joseph (Genesis 37–50)* (Leiden, 1970); A. F. Rainey (ed.), *Egypt, Israel, Sinai: Archaeological and Historical Relationships in the Biblical Period* (Tel Aviv, 1987); John Romer, *Testament: The Bible and History* (London, 1988) and Donald Redford, *Egypt, Canaan and Israel in Ancient Times* (Princeton, 1992). An English translation of Sigmund Freud's *Moses and Monotheism* is to be found in volume XXIII in James Strachey's standard edition of the *Complete Psychological Works of Sigmund Freud* (London, 1955). For the arguments against Ramesses II being the Exodus pharaoh, see Farouk Gomaa, *Chaemwese, Sohn Ramses' II. Und Hohenpriester von Memphis* (Wiesbaden, 1973).

For Flinders Petrie's system of 'sequence dating' for the Predynastic, see his own exposition of the technique in *Diospolis Parva* (London, 1901), but for a more recent approach, see Barry Kemp: 'Automatic Analysis of Predynastic Cemeteries: A New Method for an Old Problem', *Journal of Egyptian Archaeology*, 68 (1982), 5–15.

Chapter 2: Discovering and inventing

For detailed discussion of the discovery of ancient Egypt see John Wilson, *Signs and Wonders upon Pharaoh: A History of American Egyptology* (Chicago, 1964); Brian Fagan, *The Rape of the Nile: Tomb Robbers, Tourists and Archaeologists in Egypt* (New York, 1975); Peter Clayton, *The Rediscovery of Ancient Egypt: Artists and Travellers in the 19th Century* (London, 1982); Margaret Drower, *Flinders Petrie: A Life in Archaeology* (London, 1985); David O'Connor, 'Egyptology and

Archaeology: An African Perspective', in P. Robertshaw (ed.), *A History of African Archaeology* (Portsmouth and London, 1990), pp. 236–51; Jean Vercoutter, *The Search for Ancient Egypt* (London, 1992); Morris Bierbrier, *Who was Who in Egyptology*, 3rd edn. (London, 1995); Nicholas Reeves, *Ancient Egypt: The Great Discoveries* (London, 2000).

For the 'Minoan' paintings at Tell el-Dab'a see Manfred Bietak, *Avaris: The Capital of the Hyksos* (London, 1996) and Vivian Davies and Louise Schofield (eds), *Egypt, the Aegean and the Levant* (London, 1995). For the Amarna Letters see E. F. Campbell, *The Chronology of the Amarna Letters* (Baltimore, 1964); William Moran, *The Amarna Letters* (London, 1992); Shlomo Izre'el, *The Amarna Scholarly Tablets* (Groningen, 1997); Raymond Cohen and Raymond Westbrook (eds), *Amarna Diplomacy* (Baltimore and London, 2000).

For scientific techniques in Egyptology, see Alfred Lucas, *Ancient Egyptian Materials and Industries*, 4th edn. (London, 1962) and Paul Nicholson and Ian Shaw, *Ancient Egyptian Materials and Technology* (Cambridge, 2000). For Edgar Pusch's use of geophysics at Qantir see Edgar Pusch, 'Towards a Map of Piramesse', *Egyptian Archaeology*, 14 (1999), 13–15.

Chapter 3: History

The best currently available histories of ancient Egypt are Bruce Trigger, Barry Kemp, David O'Connor, and Alan Lloyd, *Ancient Egypt: A Social History* (Cambridge, 1983); Jean Vercoutter, *L'Egypte et la vallée du Nil*, i. *Des origines à la fin de l'ancien empire* (Paris, 1992); N. Grimal, *A History of Ancient Egypt* (Oxford, 1992); Claude Vandersleyen, *L'Egypte et la vallée du Nil*, ii. *De la fin de l'ancient empire à la fin du nouvel empire* (Paris, 1995); Ian Shaw (ed.), *The Oxford History of Ancient Egypt* (Oxford, 2000). There are many different sources for the chronology of ancient Egypt, but three that provide very different perspectives on the way in which the dating system has been constructed from an elaborate combination of astronomical observations, king-lists, and genealogies are Richard Parker, *The*

Calendars of Ancient Egypt (Chicago, 1950); Kenneth Kitchen, 'The Chronology of Ancient Egypt', *World Archaeology*, 23 (1991), 201–8; and Donald Redford, *Pharaonic King-lists, Annals and Day-Books: A Contribution to the Egyptian Sense of History* (Mississauga, 1986). For the Egyptians' own sense of history see John Tait (ed.), *'Never had the Like Occurred': Egypt's View of its Past* (London, 2003). For a discussion of the likely historical significance of late Predynastic votive mace-heads and palettes, see Nicholas Millett, 'The Narmer Macehead and Related Objects', *Journal of the American Research Center in Egypt*, 27 (1990), 53–9.

For Manetho, see *Manetho, Aegyptiaca*, ed. and tr. W. G. Wadell (London, 1940); for the Royal Turin Canon see Alan Gardiner, *The Royal Canon of Turin* (Oxford, 1959); and for the Palermo Stone see Toby Wilkinson, *Royal Annals of Ancient Egypt* (London, 2000). A number of problems relating to the social and political history of Egypt (many relating to the nature of the 'intermediate periods') are discussed in the following: Barbara Bell, 'The Dark Ages in Ancient History: I: The First Dark Age in Egypt', *American Journal of Archaeology*, 75 (1971), 1–26, and 'Climate and the History of Egypt: The Middle Kingdom', *American Journal of Archaeology*, 79 (1975), 223–69; Peter James, I. J. Thorpe, Nikos Kokkinos, Robert Morkot, and John Frankish, *Centuries of Darkness: A Challenge to the Conventional Chronology of Old World Archaeology* (London, 1991); William Ward, 'The Present Status of Egyptian Chronology', *Bulletin of the American Schools of Oriental Research*, 288 (1992), 53–66. For the controversy over the locations of astronomical observations used in Egyptian chronologies, see Rolf Krauss, *Sothis- und Monddaten: Studien zur astronomischen und technischen Chronologie* (Hildesheim, 1985), and for discussion of the seriation of coffins as a dating method, see Harco Willems, *Chests of Life: A Study of the Typology and Conceptual Development of Middle Kingdom Standard Class Coffins* (Leiden, 1988).

The temple at Qasr el-Sagha was published by Dieter and Dorothea Arnold in *Der Tempel Qasr el-Sagha* (Mainz, 1979), while the Middle Kingdom settlements were excavated by a Polish expedition headed by

Boleslaw Ginter and published as *Qasr el-Sagha 1980: Contributions to the Holocene Geology, the Predynastic and Dynastic Settlements in the Northern Faiyum Desert* (Warsaw and Krakow, 1983).

Chapter 4: Writing

For studies of the hieroglyphic writing system, see Alan Gardiner, *Egyptian Grammar, Being an Introduction to the Study of Hieroglyphs*, 3rd edn. (Oxford, 1957); Vivien Davies, *Egyptian Hieroglyphs* (London, 1987); Antonio Loprieno, *Ancient Egyptian: A Linguistic Introduction* (Cambridge, 1995); Mark Collier and Bill Manley, *How to Read Hieroglyphs* (London, 1998); Penelope Wilson, *Sacred Signs* (Oxford, 2003). There are several general collections of key Egyptian writings: Raymond Faulkner, *The Ancient Egyptian Pyramid Texts* (Oxford, 1969); Miriam Lichtheim, *Ancient Egyptian Literature*, 3 vols. (Berkeley, 1973–80); Edward Wente, *Letters from Ancient Egypt* (Atlanta, 1990); Richard Parkinson, *Voices from Ancient Egypt* (London, 1991). Discussions of the methods of interpreting and analysing Egyptian texts include Georges Posener, *Littérature et politique dans l'Egypte de la XII dynastie* (Paris, 1956); Antonio Loprieno (ed.), *Ancient Egyptian Literature: History and Forms* (Leiden, 1996). Papyri and ostraca, particularly of the Roman period, are discussed by R. S. Bagnall, *Reading Papyri, Writing Ancient History* (London, 1995). For the decipherment of hieroglyphs see R. Parkinson, *Cracking Codes: The Rosetta Stone and Decipherment* (London, 1999). For comparison, see also Michael Coe, *Breaking the Maya Code* (London, 1992).

For the origins of Egyptian writing, see John Ray, 'The Emergence of Writing in Egypt', *World Archaeology*, 17/3 (1986), 390–8, and Nicholas Postgate, Tao Wang, and Toby Wilkinson, 'The Evidence for Early Writing: Utilitarian or Ceremonial?', *Antiquity*, 69 (1995), 459–80.

Chapter 5: Kingship

For general discussions of Egyptian kingship see Henri Frankfort, *Kingship and the Gods* (Chicago, 1948); H. W. Fairman, 'The Kingship Rituals of Egypt', in S. H. Hooker (ed.), *Myth, Ritual and Kingship*

(Oxford, 1958), pp. 74–104; David O'Connor and David Silverman (eds.), *Ancient Egyptian Kingship* (Leiden, 1995), pp. 185–217. For Ptolemaic kingship, see E. E. Rice, *The Grand Procession of Ptolemy Philadelphus* (Oxford, 1983); K. Bringmann, 'The King as Benefactor: Some Remarks on Ideal Kingship in the Age of Hellenism', in A. Bulloch *et al.* (eds), *Images and Ideologies: Self-Definition in the Hellenistic World* (Berkeley and London, 1993). The debate concerning coregencies can be explored in William Murnane, *Ancient Egyptian Coregencies* (Chicago, 1977) and David Lorton, 'Terms of Coregency in the Middle Kingdom', *Varia Aegyptiaca*, 2 (1986), 113–20.

For Amenhotep II, see Peter der Manuelian, *Studies in the Reign of Amenophis II* (Hildesheim, 1987) and Charles Van Siclen III, *Two Monuments from the Reign of Amenhotep II* (San Antonio, 1982) and *The Alabaster Shrine of King Amenhotep II* (San Antonio, 1986).

For Hatshepsut and Senenmut, see Suzanne Ratié, *La Reine Hatchepsout* (Leiden, 1979); Joyce Tyldesley, *Hatchepsut* (London, 1998); Peter Dorman, *The Monuments of Senenmut* (London, 1988) and *The Tombs of Senenmut: The Architecture and Decoration of Tombs 71 and 353* (New York, 1991).

For Ramesses II see Kenneth Kitchen, *Pharaoh Triumphant. The Life and Times of Ramesses II, King of Egypt*, 3rd edn. (Warminster, 1985); Labib Habachi, *Features of the Deification of Ramesses II* (Glückstadt, 1969); and Joyce Tyldesley, *Ramesses: Egypt's Greatest Pharaoh* (London, 2000).

Chapter 6: Identity

For the links between the Narmer Palette and early Egyptian contact with the outside world, see Yigael Yadin, 'The Earliest Record of Egypt's Military Penetration into Asia?', *Israel Exploration Journal*, 5/1 (1955), 1–16, and see also Thomas E. Levy, Edwin C. M. van den Brink, Yuval Goren, and David Alon, 'New Light on King Narmer and the Protodynastic Egyptian presence in Canaan', *Biblical Archaeologist*, 58/1 (1995), 26–35.

For discussion of issues of Egyptian race and ethnicity, see Martin Bernal, *Black Athena: The Afro-Asiatic Roots of Classical Civilization*, 2 vols. (London, 1987–91); Frank Snowden, jun., 'Ancient Views of Nubia and the Nubians', *Expedition*, 35 (1993), 40–50; Anthony Leahy, 'Ethnic Diversity in Ancient Egypt', in J. M. Sasson (ed.) *Civilizations of the Ancient Near East* (New York, 1995), pp. 225–34; John Baines, 'Contextualizing Egyptian Representations of Society and Ethnicity', in J. S. Cooper and G. M. Schwartz (eds), *The Study of the Ancient Near East in the Twenty-First Century: The William Foxwell Albright Centennial Conference* (Winona Lake, 1996), pp. 339–84. On ethnicity during the Ptolemaic period, see Naphthali Lewis, *Greeks in Ptolemaic Egypt* (Oxford, 1986); K. Goudriaan, *Ethnicity in Ptolemaic Egypt* (Amsterdam, 1988); P. Bilde *et al.*, *Ethnicity in Hellenistic Egypt* (Aarhus, 1992).

For gender studies in Egyptology, see Lana Troy, *Patterns of Queenship in Ancient Egyptian Myth and History* (Uppsala, 1986); Barbara Lesko (ed.), *Women's Earliest Records from Ancient Egypt and Western Asia* (Atlanta, 1989); Gay Robins, *Women in Ancient Egypt* (London, 1993); Joyce Tyldesley, *Daughters of Isis: Women of Ancient Egypt* (London, 1994); Dorothea Arnold, *The Royal Women of Amarna* (New York, 1996). For sexuality, see Lise Manniche, *Sexual Life in Ancient Egypt* (London, 1987); Dominic Montserrat, *Sex and Society in Graeco-Roman Egypt* (London, 1996); Tom Hare, *ReMembering Osiris* (Stanford, Calif., 1999).

Chapter 7: Death

For Osiris, see J. Gwyn Griffiths, *The Origins of Osiris and his Cult* (Leiden, 1980). There is no shortage of books on death and mummification in ancient Egypt: Rosalie David, and E. Tapp (eds), *Evidence Embalmed: Modern Medicine and the Mummies of Ancient Egypt* (Manchester, 1984); Erik Hornung, *The Valley of the Kings* (New York 1990); Rosalie David and E. Tapp (eds), *The Mummy's Tale: The Scientific and Medical Investigation of Natsef-Amun, Priest in the Temple of Karnak* (London, 1992); Nicholas Reeves and Richard Wilkinson, *The Complete Valley of the Kings* (London, 1996);

M. Lehner, *The Complete Pyramids* (London, 1997); Salima Ikram and Aidan Dodson, *The Mummy in Ancient Egypt* (London, 1998); John Taylor, *Death and the Afterlife in Ancient Egypt* (London, 2001).

For the 'mummy's curse' see, with varying degrees of credulity and excitability, Philip Vandenberg, *The Curse of the Pharaohs* (New York, 1975) and Y. Naud, *The Curse of the Pharaohs* (Geneva, 1977). See also N. Daly, 'That Obscure Object of Desire: Victorian Commodity Culture and Fictions of the Mummy', NOVEL, 28 (1994), 24–51, for an interpretation of the popularity of mummy tales in Victorian and Edwardian times.

Chapter 8: Religion

Some earlier works on Egyptian religion and ideology are still important, e.g. Henri Frankfort, *Kingship and the Gods* (Chicago, 1948) and Siegfried Morenz, *Egyptian Religion* (London, 1973), but the best of the works published over the last 15 years are: A. I. Sadek, *Popular Religion in Ancient Egypt during the New Kingdom* (Hildesheim, 1988); W. Kelly Simpson (ed.), *Religion and Philosophy in Ancient Egypt* (New Haven, 1989); Byron E. Shafer (ed.), *Religion in Ancient Egypt: Gods, Myths and Personal Practice* (London, 1991); Jan Assmann, *Egyptian Solar Religion in the New Kingdom: Re, Amun and the Crisis of Polytheism* (London and New York, 1995); Erik Hornung, *Conceptions of God in Ancient Egypt* (Ithaca, 1982) and *Idea into Image: Essays on Ancient Egyptian Thought* (New York, 1992); Stephen Quirke, *Ancient Egyptian Religion* (London, 1992); Tom Hare, *ReMembering Osiris* (Stanford, Calif., 1999); Christopher Eyre, *The Cannibal Hymn: A Cultural and Literary Study* (Liverpool, 2002). For discussion of the early monuments at Nabta Playa, see Fred Wendorf, Romuald Schild, and Nieves Zedeno, 'A Late Neolithic Megalith Complex in the Eastern Sahara: A Preliminary Report', in L. Krzyzaniak (ed.), *Interregional Contacts in the Later Prehistory of Northeastern Africa* (Poznan, 1996), 125–32, and for the early temple at Hierakonpolis, see Reneé Friedman, 'The Ceremonial Centre at Hierakonpolis Locality HK29A', in A.J. Spencer (ed.) *Aspects of Early Egypt* (London, 1993), 16–35.

Chapter 9: Egyptomania: the recycling and reinventing of Egypt's icons and images

For a discussion of some of the theories concerning the nature and purpose of pyramids see Lynn Picknett and Clive Prince, 'Alternative Egypts', in S. MacDonald and M. Rice (eds.), *Consuming Ancient Egypt* (London, 2003), pp. 175–94. For Charles Piazzi Smyth's contribution to pyramidology, see *Life and Work at the Great Pyramid* (London, 1867).

For Akhenaten and the Amarna period see Donald Redford, *Akhenaten: The Heretic King* (Princeton, 1984); Cyril Aldred, *Akhenaten, King of Egypt* (London, 1988); William Murnane, *Texts from the Amarna Period in Egypt* (Atlanta, 1995); Erik Hornung, *Akhenaten and the Religion of Light* (Ithaca, 1997); Dominic Montserrat, *Akhenaten: History, Fantasy and Ancient Egypt* (London, 2000); Nicholas Reeves, *Akhenaten: Egypt's False Prophet* (London, 2001).

For Nefertiti see Julia Samson, *Nefertiti and Cleopatra: Queen-Monarchs of Ancient Egypt* (London, 1985) and Joyce Tyldesley, *Nefertiti: Egypt's Sun Queen* (London, 1998).

For Cleopatra see Michael Grant, *Cleopatra* (London, 1972); Richard Fazzini and Robert Bianchi, *Cleopatra's Egypt* (New York, 1981); Lucy Hughes-Hallett, *Cleopatra: Histories, Dreams and Distortions* (London, 1990); Mary Hamer, *Signs of Cleopatra: History, Politics, Representation* (London and New York, 1993); Susan Walker and Peter Higgs, *Cleopatra of Egypt: From History to Myth* (London, 2001).

For 'alternative' views of the Egyptian evidence, see Lynn Picknett and Clive Prince, The Stargate Conspiracy: Revealing the Truth behind Extraterrestrial Contact, Military Intelligence and the Mysteries of *Ancient Egypt* (London, 2000).

Useful websites

Organizations, institutions, and general Egyptological websites

http://www.asor.org (American Society for Oriental Research)

http://www.newton.cam.ac.uk/egypt/ (very useful general Egyptological site, based in Cambridge UK, providing numerous hypertext links to other sites)

http://www.uk.sis.gov.eg/online/ (Egyptian government information on current archaeological work in Egypt)

http://www.ashmol.ox.ac.uk/gri/ (the Griffith Institute and the Topographical Bibliography)

http://www.ancientneareast.net/sites.html (general site on the Near East)

http://www.benben.de (German-language site, mainly about pyramids)

http://www.digitalegypt.ucl.ac.uk (an excellent undergraduate-level information resource, based around the Petrie Museum collection in London)

http://www.ees.ac.uk (the Egypt Exploration Society, the main coordinator of British archaeological work in Egypt)

http://www.leidenuniv.nl/nino/aeb.html (the Annual Egyptological Bibliography)

http://www.leidenuniv.nl/nino/dmd/dmd.html (a Deir el-Medina database)

http://www.bbaw.de/forschung/altaegyptwb/ (the Altägyptisches

Wörterbuch, a comprehensive on-line dictionary of the ancient Egyptian language)

http://www.sas.upenn.edu/African_Studies/Articles_Gen/ afrocent_roth.html (an excellent site devoted to the discussion of afrocentrism)

http://www.eeescience.utoledo.edu/faculty/harrell/egypt/Quarries/ (a site concerned primarily with geology and use of stone in ancient Egypt)

Current excavations and surveys

http://www.kv5.com (Kent Weeks's excavation of KV5 in the Valley of the Kings)

http://www.valleyofthekings.org/vofk/ (current work in the Valley of the Kings)

www.franckgoddio.org/ (French marine archaeology in the harbour at Alexandria)

http://www.pbs.org/wgbh/nova/pyramid/excavation/ (Mark Lehner's work at Giza)

http://www.mcdonald.cam.ac.uk/Projects/Amarna/ (Barry Kemp's survey and excavations at Amarna)

http://www.hierakonpolis.org/hk.html (Renée Friedman's excavations at Hierakonpolis)

Museums

http://www.egyptianmuseum.gov.eg/ (Egyptian Museum, Cairo)

http://www.mfa.org/egypt (Museum of Fine Arts, Boston)

http://www.metmuseum.org/collections/department.asp?dep = 10 (Metropolitan Museum, New York)

http://www.brooklynart.org (Brooklyn Museum, New York)

http://www-oi.uchicago.edu/OI/MUS/GALLERY/EGYPT/ New_Egypt_Gallery.html (Oriental Institute Museum, Chicago)

http://www.thebritishmuseum.ac.uk/egypt/museum.html (British Museum, London)

http://www.petrie.ucl.ac.uk (Petrie Museum of Egyptian Archaeology at University College London)

http://www.louvre.fr/francais/collec/ae/ae_f.html (Louvre, Paris) http://www.museoegizio.org/ (Museo Egizio, Turin)

http://www.smb.spk-berlin.de/amp (Egyptian Museum, Berlin)

http://www.museum.man.ac.uk/ (Manchester Museum, UK)

http://www.ashmol.ox.ac.uk/ (Ashmolean Museum, Oxford)

http://www.fitzmuseum.cam.ac.uk/ (Fitzwilliam Museum, Cambridge)

http://www.rmo.nl/ (Rijksmuseum van Oudheden, Leiden)

http://www.amarna.com (the Mansoor collection, see Chapter 9, p. 146)

Glossary

akh: one of the five principal elements that the Egyptians considered necessary to make up a complete personality (the other four being the *ka, ba,* name, and shadow). It was believed to be both the form in which the blessed dead inhabited the underworld, and also the result of the successful reunion of the *ba* with its *ka*.

Aten: deity represented in the form of the disc or orb of the sun, the cult of which was particularly promoted during the reign of Akhenaten.

*ba, ba-***bird:** aspect of human beings that resembles our concept of 'personality', comprising the non-physical attributes which made each person unique. The *ba* was often depicted as a bird with a human head and arms, and was also used to refer to the physical manifestations of certain gods.

bark, bark shrine: The bark was an elaborate type of boat used to transport the cult images of Egyptian gods from one shrine to another. The bark shrine was a stone structure in which the bark could be temporarily set down as it was being carried in ritual processions from one temple to another during festivals.

Books of the Netherworld/Book of the Dead: The netherworld texts comprise a number of related funerary writings, which together were known to the Egyptians as Amduat or 'that which is in the Netherworld'. They included the *Book of Caverns*, *Book of Gates*, and the *Writing of the Hidden Chamber*. The theme of all of these works is the journey of the sun-god through the realms of darkness during the 12 hours of the night, leading up to his triumphant rebirth with the dawn each morning. The above examples were found in royal tombs primarily during the New Kingdom, but a more widespread example, known from the Second Intermediate Period onwards, was the *Book of Dead*, frequently inscribed on papyrus and placed with both royal and non-royal burials.

BP: abbreviation for 'before present', which is most commonly used for uncalibrated radiocarbon dates or thermoluminescence dates. 'Present' is conventionally taken to be AD 1950.

cartouche (*shenu*): elliptical outline representing a length of knotted rope with which certain elements of the Egyptian royal titulary were surrounded from the 4th Dynasty onwards.

cenotaph: literally meaning 'empty tomb', this term is usually applied to buildings constructed to celebrate an individual's funerary cult but containing no human remains.

Coffin Texts: group of over a thousand spells, selections from which were inscribed on coffins during the Middle Kingdom.

demotic: cursive script (Greek, 'popular (script)') known to the Egyptians as *sekh shat*, which replaced the *hieratic* script by the 26th Dynasty. Initially used only in commercial and bureaucratic documents, by the Ptolemaic period it was also being used for religious, scientific and literary texts.

Glossary

faience: glazed non-clay ceramic material widely used in Egypt for the production of such items as jewellery, *shabtis* and vessels.

false door: stone or wooden architectural element comprising a rectangular imitation door placed inside Egyptian non-royal tomb-chapels. Funerary offerings were usually placed in front of false doors.

hieratic: cursive script used from at least the end of the Early Dynastic period onwards, enabling scribes to write more rapidly on papyri and ostraca, making it the preferred medium for scribal tuition (Greek *hieratika*, 'sacred'). An even more cursive form of the script, known as 'abnormal hieratic', began to be used for business texts in Upper Egypt during the Third Intermediate Period.

hieroglyphics: script consisting of pictograms, ideograms and phonograms arranged in horizontal and vertical lines (Greek, 'sacred carved (letters)'), which was in use from the late Gerzean period (*c.*3200 BC) to the late 4th century AD.

Horus name: the first royal name in the sequence of five names making up the Egyptian royal titulary, usually written inside a *serekh*.

instruction: type of literary text (e.g. *The Instruction of Amenemhat I*) consisting of aphorisms and ethical advice (Egyptian *sebayt*, 'wisdom texts', 'didactic literature').

ka: the creative life-force of any individual, whether human or divine. Represented by a hieroglyph consisting of a pair of arms, it was considered to be the essential ingredient that differentiated a living person from a dead one.

Maat: goddess symbolizing justice, truth, and universal harmony, usually depicted either as an ostrich feather or as a seated woman wearing such a feather on her head.

mastaba-**tomb:** type of Egyptian tomb, the rectangular superstructure of which resembles the low mud-brick benches outside Egyptian houses (Arabic, 'bench'). It was used for both royal and non-royal burials in the Early Dynastic Period but only for non-royal burials from the Old Kingdom onwards.

Maya: Mesoamerican people and culture who flourished *c.*AD 200–850.

nome: Greek term used to refer to the 42 traditional provinces of Egypt, which the ancient Egyptians themselves called *sepat*. For most of the dynastic period, there were 22 Upper Egyptian and 20 Lower Egyptian nomes.

nomen: birth name; royal name introduced by the epithet *sa-Ra* ('son of Ra'). Usually the last one in the sequence of the *royal titulary*, it was the only one given to the pharaoh as soon as he was born.

offering formula: prayer asking for offerings to be brought to the deceased, which formed the focus of food offerings in non-royal tombs (*hetep-di-nesw* 'a gift which the king gives'). The formula is often accompanied by a depiction of the deceased sitting in front of an offering table heaped with food.

Opening of the Mouth ceremony: funerary ritual by which the deceased and his funerary statuary were brought to life.

ostracon: sherds of pottery or flakes of limestone bearing texts and drawings, commonly consisting of personal jottings, letters, sketches or scribal exercises, but sometimes also inscribed with literary texts, usually in the *hieratic* script (Greek *ostrakon*, pl. *ostraka*; 'potsherd').

playa: plain or depression where run-off from surrounding highlands collects, forming an ephemeral lake. When dry, the playa, sometimes containing archaeological deposits, is subject to aeolian processes of erosion and deposition.

prenomen: throne name; one of the five names in the Egyptian *royal titulary*, which was introduced by the title *nesu-bit*: 'he of the sedge and the bee', which is a reference both to the individual mortal king and the eternal kingship (not 'king of Upper and Lower Egypt', as it is sometimes erroneously translated).

pylon: massive ceremonial gateway (Greek, 'gate'), called *bekhenet* by the Egyptians, which consisted of two tapering towers linked by a bridge of masonry and surmounted by a cornice. It was used in temples from at least the Middle Kingdom to the Roman period.

Pyramid Texts: the earliest Egyptian funerary texts, comprising some 800 spells or 'utterances' written in columns on the walls of the corridors and burial chambers of nine pyramids of the late Old Kingdom and First Intermediate Period.

quern-stone: a large stone used for grinding cereals such as wheat or barley. The two most common types are the 'saddle quern', which has a concave upper surface, and the 'rotary quern', in which one stone is rotated over another.

***rekhyt* bird:** Egyptian term for the lapwing (*Vanellus vanellus*), a type of plover with a characteristic crested head, often used as a symbol for foreigners or subject peoples.

royal titulary: classic sequence of names and titles held by each of the pharaohs consisting of five names (the so-called 'fivefold titulary'), which was not fully established until the Middle Kingdom. It consisted of the Horus name, the Golden Horus name, the Two Ladies name (*nebty*), the birth name (nomen, *sa-Ra*) and the throne-name (prenomen, *nesu-bit*).

satrapy: province in the Achaemenid (Persian) Empire.

scarab: type of seal found in Egypt, Nubia and Syria-Palestine from the 11th Dynasty until the Ptolemaic period. Its name derives from the fact that it was carved in the shape of the sacred scarab beetle (*Scarabaeus sacer*).

sed-festival: royal ritual of renewal and regeneration, which was intended to be celebrated by the king only after a reign of 30 years had elapsed (*heb-sed*, royal jubilee).

serekh: rectangular panel (perhaps representing a palace gateway) surmounted by the Horus falcon (or the Seth jackal), within which the king's 'Horus name' was written.

seriation: method of arranging artefacts, sites, or assemblages into a linear sequence on the basis of the degree of similarity between the various elements in the sequence (e.g. developments in artefactual style, function, or material).

shabti, ushabti, shawabti: funerary figurine, usually mummiform in appearance, which developed during the Middle Kingdom out of the funerary statuettes and models provided in the tombs of the Old Kingdom. The purpose of the statuettes was to perform menial labour for their owners in the afterlife.

sistrum: musical rattling instrument (Egyptian *seshesht*; Greek *seistron*) played mainly by women, but also by the pharaoh when making offerings to the goddess Hathor.

solar boat, solar bark: boat in which the sun-god and the deceased pharaoh travelled through the netherworld; there were two different types: that of the day (*mandet*), and that of the night (*mesektet*).

sphinx: mythical beast usually portrayed with the body of a lion and the head of a man, often wearing the royal *nemes* headcloth, as in the case of the Great Sphinx at Giza. Statues of sphinxes were also sometimes given the heads of rams (criosphinxes) or hawks (hierakosphinxes).

talatat blocks: small sandstone or limestone relief blocks dating to the Amarna period, the name for which probably derives from the Arabic for 'three hand-breadths', describing their dimensions (although the word may also have stemmed from the Italian *tagliata*, 'cut masonry').

Two Ladies name: one of the royal names in the 'fivefold titulary'; the term (*nebty*) derives from the fact that this name was under the protection of two goddesses: Nekhbet and Wadjet.

vizier: term used to refer to the holders of the Egyptian title *tjaty*, whose position is considered to have been roughly comparable with that of the vizier (or chief minister) in the Ottoman Empire. The vizier was therefore usually the next most powerful person after the king.

Timeline

Prehistory

Palaeolithic	*c.*700,000–10,000 BP
Epipalaeolithic	*c.*10,000–7000 BP
Neolithic	*c.*5300–4000 BC
Maadi Cultural Complex (north only)	*c.*4000–3200
Badarian period	*c.*4500–3800
Amratian (Naqada I) period	*c.*4000–3500
Gerzean (Naqada II) period	*c.*3500–3200
Naqada III/'Dynasty 0'	*c.*3200–3000

Pharaonic/Dynastic Period 3000–332 BC

Early Dynastic Period 3000–2686

1st Dynasty	3000–2890
2nd Dynasty	2890–2686

Old Kingdom 2686–2181

3rd Dynasty	2686–2613
4th Dynasty	2613–2494
5th Dynasty	2494–2345
6th Dynasty	2345–2181

First Intermediate Period 2181–2055

7th and 8th Dynasties	2181–2125
9th and 10th Dynasties	2160–2025
11th Dynasty (Thebes only)	2125–2055

Middle Kingdom 2055–1650

11th Dynasty (all Egypt)	2055–1985
12th Dynasty	1985–1795
13th Dynasty	1795-after 1650
14th Dynasty	1750–1650

Second Intermediate Period 1650–1550

15th Dynasty (Hyksos)	1650–1550
16th Dynasty (minor Hyksos)	1650–1550
17th Dynasty (Theban)	1650–1550

New Kingdom 1550–1069

18th Dynasty	1550–1295
Ramessid period	1295–1069
19th Dynasty	1295–1186
20th Dynasty	1186–1069

Third Intermediate Period 1069–664

21st Dynasty	1069–945
22nd Dynasty	945–715
23rd Dynasty	818–715
24th Dynasty	727–715
25th Dynasty (Kushite)	747–656

Late Period 664–332

26th Dynasty (Saite)	664–525
27th Dynasty (1st Persian period)	525–404
28th Dynasty	404–399
29th Dynasty	399–380
30th Dynasty	380–343
2nd Persian period	343–332

Ptolemaic Period 332–30 BC

Macedonian Dynasty	332–305
Cleopatra VII Philopator	51–30

Roman Period 30 BC–AD 311

Index

Page references in *italics* refer to illustrations.

A

Abu Simbel graffiti 15
Abydos:
  cemeteries 40, 49–50, 54, 60, 63,
    76–8, 82, 113
  Osiris cult 115, 118–19
  temple of Seti I 117
Abydosfahrt 118–19
Actium, Battle of (31 BC) 154
Aegyptiaca 60, 62
Africa 103
Afrocentrism 106–7, 138, 151
afterlife 112, 115, 119, 120–1, 135
Aha 60, 113, 114
Ahmose 94
akh element 120, 121
Akhenaten 19, 36, 145–9
Akhetaten *see* Amarna period
Akkadians 7–8, 36, 39
Alashiya, kingdom of 38–9
Alcott, Louisa May 125
Alexander the Great 64
Alexandria 12, 156
Ali, Mohammed, Viceroy of Egypt 97
Amarna excavation (1891–2) 24–5, 36
Amarna Letters 32, 35–9
Amarna period 19, 145–54
Amélineau, Emile 23, 114
Amenemhat I 136
Amenemhat II 56, 59
Amenemhat III 66, *86*
Amenemhat IV 66
Amenemhet, governor 119
Amenhotep II 87–8
Amenhotep III 15, 36, 41, 93–4
Amenhotep IV *see* Akhenaten
Amenmes, priest 60
Amman, city of 103
Amun, god 93, 94, 133
Amunherkhepeshef, son of Ramesses
  II 17
Anatolia 103
Anaximander 12
Andjety, god 115

animal sacrifices 114, 132
Ankhtifi, governor 135
Anksheshonqy 136
Antony, Mark 154
Anubis, god of the underworld 129
Aper-el, vizier 105
'Apiru people 37
Apperson, Phoebe 24
Arabia 103
archaeology 11
  biblical 20
  'clearance' of sites 23–4
  culture history approach 50
  death and the afterlife 120
  evidence of women's lives 110
  innovative methods 24–5
  Napoleonic 20
  sacred state structures 24, 129, 132
  textual evidence and 79–81, 88,
    132–3
  trends in 26–7
Arnold, Dieter and Dorothea 66
art:
  Amarna period 146, 148, 149–54
  androcentrism 108
  characteristic features of 7
  commemorative 54–5
  ethnicity and 105
  Minoan 32, 34–5
  Osiris and Isis myth 117
  phallocentrism 133
  religious 127–8
  tomb 34, 82, 105, 108, *109*, 119 *see*
    also iconography
Asante, Molefi Kete 106
Ashmolean Museum, Oxford 133
Asia 103
Asiatics 6, 98, 105–6
Assmann, Jan 19, 99–100
Assyrians 16, 36
astronomy 63, 69, 131, 141–2
Asyut coffins *69*, 70
Aten, god 19, 145
Atum, god 100, 111
Avaris, city of 34

B

ba element 120, 121, 123, 142
Bactrians 96
Badarian culture 122
Bak, royal sculptor 146
Bakhtan, kingdom of 96

Balderston, John 124
basalt 67
Bastet, cat-goddess 13
Bat, cow-goddess 107, 126, 127, 131
Battlefield Palette 4
Bauval, Robert 142, 158
Belzoni, Giovanni 23, 97
Bentresh Stele 96-7
Berlin Egyptian Museum 36, 115, 151, 153
Bernal, Martin 104, 106, 138, 158
Bible 16-20, 107, 141, 142-3
Bietak, Manfred 34-5
Binford, Lewis 26
bit loaves 132-3
Boccaccio, Giovanni 154
Borchardt, Ludwig 151
Brace, C. Loring 107
Breasted, James Henry 111
British Museum 36, 38, 97
Bronze Age 35-6
Brooklyn Museum 39
Bubastis 78
Budge, Wallis 35, 111
bulls:
  and kingship 5, 6, 85, 87, 88, 102, 131-2
  Minoan art 34
bureaucracy 75-6, 78
burials 41, 49-50, 114, 131 *see also* cemeteries; coffins; tombs
Burridge, Alwyn 147
Burton, Richard *155*
Buto 78
Byblos, port of 117

C

Campbell, Colin 93-4
Canaan 37
captives 5-8, 6, 55, 82, 101, 102, 103-4, 134
Carnarvon, Lord 124, 158
Carnarvon Tablet 56
Carter, Howard 40-1, 158
cartography 12
Ceasarion, son of Cleopatra 157
cedar-wood 117
cemeteries 40, 49-50, 54, 60, 63, 76-7, 82, 113-14, 122
ceramics *see* pottery
Chabas, François 79
Champollion, Jean-François xi, 59, 79

Childe, Gordon 107
China 75
Christie, Agatha 159
chronology 58-67, 70
cinema 18, 124, 142, 149, 154, 156, 158
Cleopatra VII 94, 154-7
Coffin Texts 121
coffins 58, 69-70
colossi 14-15, 96, 97, 133
Conan Doyle, Sir Arthur 123
Coptic script 79
co-regencies 63
creation myths 99-100, 133, 143
Crete 34-5, 103
culture 7, 50, 63-4, 68-9, 75
cuneiform writing 32, 35, 76
cylinders 55
Cyprus 38-9, 103

D

Daly, N. 123-4
dating methods 24, 25, 58
  Middle Kingdom coffins 69-70
  pottery 68-9
  Qasr el-Sagha case-study 65-7
  sequence dating 26, 40, 48-9
Davis, Whitney 108
de Morgan, Jacques 23, 40
death 114, 119-21
Deir-el-Bahari temple 89, 93
Deir el-Medina tomb scene *109*
deities 111, 117, 126-9, 133 *see also under* individual names
Delta excavations 141
DeMille, Cecil B. 18, 156
demotic script xi, 79, 136
Den 60
Dendera 117
Der Manuelian, Peter 88
Deshret ('red country') 10 ·
Diels, Herman 13
diffusionism 98, 106-7
Diodorus Siculus 12, 14, 96, 97
Diop, Cheikh Anta 104, 106, 138
diplomacy 37-8
dismemberment 117, 118, 121, 122
divine birth myth 93-4
Djedkara Isesi 135
Djedu (later Busiris) 115
Djer 60, 114
Djet 60
Djoser 143

DNA sampling 43
Dreyer, Günter 55
Drovetti, Bernardino 23, 59
Dynastic Race ('Followers of Horus')
  6, 50

E

Eannatum Victory Stele 7
Early Dynastic period 29, 44, 48, 49,
  54, 113–14
Edwards, Amelia 24, 98–9
Edwards, I. E. S. 158
Egypt Exploration Society 98, 141
Egyptian Museum, Cairo 36, 42, 44,
  58, 60, 114
Egyptology/Egyptologists 20, 23–8
  Afrocentrism 106–7, 138, 151
  alternative 142, 157–8
  chronology 58–67
  data interpretation 39–40, 45–6,
    137, 139–44
  decipherment of hieroglyphs 79
  gender studies 107–12
  media response to 32, 33
  modern 137–8
  popularizing 40–1, 144–59
  religious questions 129, 131
  science and 42–7
  stereotyping pharaohs 87–100
Elephantine 39, 40, 63
Emery, Bryan 49, 50, 107
Ennead 99
ethnicity 97–8, 102–7, 154, 156
eugenics movement 107
Exodus narrative 17–19
Ezbet Helmi palace 34

F

Fairservis, jnr, Walter 74
Faiyum region 64, 66
famine 135
Faulkner, Raymond 111
fertility 111, 115, 117
fieldwork 25, 26, 27–8, 43–4
Fiorelli, Guiseppe 25
First Intermediate Period 69, 70–1,
  135, 136
fivefold titulary 85
frescos (Tell el-Dab'a) 32, 34–5
Freud, Sigmund 19
Froehlich's Syndrome 147

funerary texts 118, 121, 126, 134–5,
  143

G

Gardin, Jean-Claude 80, 81
Gardiner, Alan 74, 87, 90
Gautier, Théophile 123
Gebel Qatrani quarries 67
gender 107–11
geography 11–12
geological analysis 44–7
geophysics 43
Giza 141–3, 158
Glass, Philip 149, 158
Gomaa, Farouk 17–18
Goodwin, Charles 79
Goren, Dr Yuval 38–9
graffiti 14–15, 60
grave goods 40, 121
Great Harris Papyrus 56
Great Pyramid at Giza 43, 141–3, 158
Greeks 11–15, 103
Green, Frederick 82
greywacke 44, 45
Grimal, Nicolas 87, 90, 92

H

Hadad the Edomite 16
Haggard, Rider 123, 124
Hamad desert 103
Hamer, Mary 156
Hamilton, William 97
Hammamat siltstone 44–5
Hancock, Graham 142
Hardjedef 135, 136
Hare, Tom 8, 112, 133
Haremhab 91
Harkhuf 135
Harpy, god 146–7
Hathor, cow-goddess 117, 126, 131
Hatshepsut, Queen 18–19, 56, 89–94,
  98, 108, 110
Hayes, William 56
Hebrews see Israelites
Hecataeus of Abdera 14, 96
Hecataeus of Miletus 12, 13
Heliopolis 63, 158
Herodotus 12–13, 57, 95, 107, 118,
  122
Hetepheres, mother of Khufu 110
Hierakonpolis 50, 82, 113

Early Dynastic sculpture 44
'main deposit' artefacts 1, 29–30, 52
Predynastic period 121, 132
hieratic script 79
hieroglyphics xi, 72
    decipherment of 79
    Narmer label 55
    Narmer Palette 73–4, 103
    Palermo Stone inscription 58–9
    use of 75–8
Hilliard III, Asa G. 151–2
Hitler, Adolf 151
Hittites 36, 96, 97
ḥm signs 5, 6
Hoffman, Michael 30
Homer 11
Honorius, Julius 141
Horace 154
Horeau, Hector 23
Hornung, Erik 57, 126–7, 136, 145
Horus, falcon-god 6, 50, 58, 84, 99,
    100, 101, 117, 129, 134
Horus name *see serekh* symbols
Hosea, king of Samaria 16
housing 66, 110
human sacrifice 40, 134
Hunt, Leigh 97
Hurrian language 36
Hyksos 19, 56, 60
hyper-diffusionism 98

I

iconography 6–7, 73, 82, 101–5, 108,
    132, 134
ideograms 6, 72, 73–4, 103–4
ideology 54–6, 134–6
Ikhernofret, priest 115
Instruction of Amenemipet 19–20
Intermediate periods 34, 59, 60,
    62–3, 69, 70–1, 95, 122, 135, 136
inundations 10, 12, 59, 115, 147
Iri-Hor, tomb of 113, 114
Iroquoian Native Americans 7
irrigation canals 53
Isis, goddess xi, 117–18
Israel 104
Israelites 17, 37, 143
ivory artefacts 29, 54–5, 102

J

Jacq, Christian 98
Jeffreys, David 158

Jerusalem 16
Jews *see* Israelites 17
Jones, Jana 122
Joseph 17, 141
Josephus 60

K

Ka, tomb of 113, 114
ka element 120, 121, 123
Kahun, pyramid-town of 66
Kamose stelae 56, 57
Karloff, Boris 124, 158
Karnak 96, 145
Karnak King-List 60
Keats, John 97
Kemet ('black land') 10, 106
Kemp, Barry 9, 67, 81, 129, 143–4
Khafra, statue of *84*
Khasekhemwy 44
khaty-bity ritual 52
Khepri, sun-god 129
Khnumhotep II, governor 119
Khonsu, god 96, 97
Khufu *see* Great Pyramid
king-lists 58–62, 70
kingship 14, 50
    bull symbol and 5, 6, 85, 87, 88,
        102, 131–2
    divine birth myth 93–4
    female 89–94, 110, 152, 154–7
    imitation of acts of 119
    religion and 133–4
    rituals of 52, 53, 55–6
    'smoting' iconography *2*, 6–7, 73,
        82–3, 101, 102, 134
    stereotypes 87–100
    titles of 4, 55, 73–4, 85, 88, 105
Kitchen, Kenneth 99
Kom Rabi'a site, Memphis 68
Koptos excavation 133
Krauss, Rolf 63
Kushites 15

L

labels 54–5, 76, *77*, 78
Lahun 63
Late Dynastic Period 29
Laughlin, John 18, 37
Levant 34, 103–4
Libya 55, 103
life expectancy 63

lions 114
Lloyd, Alan 13
Loudon, Jane Webb 123
Louvre 36
Lower Egypt (northern region) 5, 10, 13, 49, 58, 78, 101
Lucas, Alfred 42
Lucian 15–16
Lupton, Carter 123
Luxor *see* Thebes

M

Ma-hor-neferura, princess 97
Maat 99, 136
Mace, Arthur 69, 70
mace-heads 5, 29, *51*, 52–4, 104, 113
magnetometry 43, 44
Maiherpri, military official 105
Malek, Jaromir 152
Malraux, André 154
Manetho 12, 60, 62
Mann, Thomas 145
Marfan's Syndrome 147
masks 129
Mayans 8, 75, 80
Medamud shrine 66
Medinet Habu temple 95, 132
Medinet Maadi temple 66
Mediterranean region 26, 103
Memnon colossi 14–15
Memphis 56, 59, 68, 69
Menes 58, 59
Mentuhotep II 69
Merenptah 18, 98
Merikara 135
Merneith 60
Meskell, Lynn 111–12
Mesolithic period 10
Mesopotamia 3, 4, 50, 75, 76, 102, 103
Middle Kingdom 30, 56–7, 59
    coffins 69–70
    female ruler 89, 110
    Osiris cult 118–19
    settlements 66–7
    temples 65–6
military expansionism 103–4
Millet, Nick 53, 55
Min, god 133
Minoan frescos 32, 34–5
Mitrahina day-book 59

Momos, god 15–16
monotheism 19, 127, 145
Monthu, god 66
mortuary temples 15, 96
Moses 19
mummies 85, 112, 117, 120, 129
    evolution of 121–3
    examination of 43, 98
    Osiris and 116
    popular fiction and film 123–5
Murray, Margaret 149
Museo Egizio, Turin 59
Mycenaean culture 34
myth 57, 93–4, 99–100, 117–18, 133, 143

N

Nabta Playa site 131
Naga ed-Der cemetery 25
Naqada period 5, 40, 48, 132
nar-mer signs 73
Narmer 60, 113
Narmer cylinder 55, 102
Narmer ivory label 54–5, 102
Narmer mace-head *51*, 52, 53
Narmer Palette 1, *2, 3*, 4–9, 29, 30, 55
    Bat goddess 126
    gender 107–8
    Horus 134
    interpretation of 48–9, 137
    kingship 6–7, 82, 84, 85, 134
    military expansionism theory 103–4
    origins of Egyptian writing 73–4
    scientific analysis of 44–6
    smiting scene *2*, 6–7, 73, 82, 101, 102, 134
Naville, Professor Edouard 13, *140*
Nefertiti, Queen 94, 110, 145, 147, 148
    bust of 149, *150*, 151–4
Neferura, princess 96
Neferure, daughter of Hatshepsut 92, 94
Neolithic period 10, 122, 131
Nephthys 116
New Kingdom 15, 17, 58, 93, 122, 145–9
Nile inundations 10, 12, 59, 115, 147
Ningirsu, god 7
Nubia 90, 103, 105
Nut, god 69

Index

O

O'Connor, David 27, 81
offerings 132–5
officials 5, 105, 135
Old Kingdom 29, 30, 58, 59, 68, 85, 110, 117–18
Old Testament 16–20
Opening of the mouth ritual 73
opera 149, 158
Orion 141–2
Osiris, cult of 100, 114–19, 121, 122
OSL (optically stimulated luminescence) 58, 65, 68
Osorkon 16, 56
ostracon 128
Osymandias 96
Otto, Eberhard 145
'Ozymandias' (Shelley) 97

P

Paglia, Camille 152
Palaeolithic period 10
Palermo Stone 53, 58–9
Palestine 36–7, 56, 103–4, 117
palettes see Narmer Palette
papyri 6–7, 18, 39–40, 56, 59–60, 62, 79, 136
Peet, Eric 42
Pepi I 29
Persians 16
Petrie, Flinders 48
    Abydos excavation 114
    Amarna excavation 24–5, 36
    Delta site excavations 141
    invasion theory 40, 106–7
    Koptos excavation 133
    Naqada cemeteries 40
    personal geological categorization 46
    sequence dating 26, 40, 48–9
Petrie Museum, University College London 58, 114
petroglyphs 132
petrology 38–9, 43
phallocentrism 111, 117, 133
Philae, island of xi
Phoenician papyrus rolls 39–40
phonetic signs 72, 73, 78
Piazzi Smyth, Charles 142–3
pilgrimage 114, 118–19
Piye stele 56

Plutarch 116–17, 154
Poe, Edgar Allen 123
politics 64–5, 68–9
popular fiction 123–4, 149
pottery 46–7, 63–4, 68–71, 82
Predynastic period 25, 26, 40, 48–52, 63–4
    burials 40, 49, 113, 121–2
    labels 54, 76
    mummies 121
    religion 131–3
    symbols 73–4, 82
    writing 76–7
priests 95, 97, 115, 129
propaganda 75, 76, 91, 93, 97
Propertius 154
proton-magnetometer surveys 43
Proverbs 19–20
Psalm 104 19
Psamtek I 11, 13
Psamtek II 15
Ptah temple 59
Ptahhotep, vizier 135
Ptolemaic period 64
Ptolemy, General 64
Ptolemy I 14
Ptolemy II 62
Ptolemy XII 157
Punt, kingdom of 90, 103
Pusch, Edgar 44
Putnam, Nina Wilcox 124
Pyramid Texts 121, 126, 143
pyramidology 139–44, 158
Pyrrho 14

Q

Qadesh, battle of (c.1286 BC) 96
Qantir excavation site 44
Qasr el-Sagha temple 64, 65–7
quarries 45, 60, 67
Quibell, James and Green, Frederick 1, 4, 29–31, 49, 52

R

Ra, sun-god 94
racism 98, 106–7
radiocarbon dating 58
Ramesses II 15, 17–18, 41, 59, 60, 93, 95–100
Ramesses III 56, 105
Ramesseum 96, 97

Ratié, Suzanne 93
Ray, John 148
Red Crown of Lower Egypt 5
Red Sea 19
Redford, Donald 19, 54, 56, 57, 90–2, 145
Reeves, Nicholas 148–9, 151
Reisner, George 24, 25
religion 126–33
  Egyptian writing and 73
  ideology and 134–6
  kingship and 133–4
  monotheism 19, 127, 145
  phallocentrism 111, 117, 133
  Predynastic 131–3
Renenutet, goddess 66
Renfrew, Colin 26
resistivity surveys 43
Rice, Ann 98
Rice, Michael 94
rituals 52, 53, 55–6, 73, 115, 129, 131
rock-temples 56
rock-tombs 15
Rohmer, Sax 123
Roman period 15–16, 45, 64
Romer, John 20
Rosetta Stone 1
Rosicrucianism 146

S

sacrifice 40, 114, 132, 134
Saddam Hussein 96
Sah, god 69, 142
Saite period 17
sandstone 65–6
Santorini 19, 34
Saqqara step-pyramid 143
Saqqara Tablet 60
Sayce, Archibald 35
Schiffer, Michael 26
schist 45
science 42–7, 58
Scorpion (ruler) 78
Scorpion mace-head 52–3
scribes 39
Sea Peoples 103
Sebennytos, temple of 62
Second Intermediate Period 34, 60
Seidlmayer, Stephan 70–1
Senenmut, royal steward 91, 92, 93, 94
Senusret II 62, 66

Senusret III 62, 63, 66
sequence dating 26, 40, 48–9
serekh symbol 4, 55, 73–4, 88, 104
seriation 26, 40, 68, 69–70
serpopards 3, 4, 102
Sesostris 95
Seth 116–17, 118
Seti I 60, 98, 105, 116, 117
settlements 34, 66–7, 110, 120
sexuality 111–12
Seyffarth, Gustavus 59
šd šd (shedshed) 5–6
Shelley, Percy Bysshe 97
Shoshenq I 16
siltstone 44–5
Simon, Dr James 151
Sirius, dog-star 63, 69
Smenkhkare 148
Smith, Grafton Elliot 25, 98, 106, 147
Sneferu 97
Sobekneferu, Queen 89, 110
Sokar-Osiris, shrine of 117
Sopdet, god 69
Spence, Kate 142
Speos Artemidos rock-temple 56
spinning and weaving 108
standing stones 131
star clocks 69, 70
stelae 7, 18, 53, 56, 57, 58–9, 75, 96–7, 115, 135
step pyramids 143
Stephanus of Byzantium 12
Stoker, Bram 123
Strabo 12, 15
Sumeria 76, 136
Syncellus, George 62
Syria-Palestine 36–7, 56, 103, 117

T

Taylor, Elizabeth 154, 155
Taylor, John 141, 142, 143
Tefnakht of Sais 16
Tell Basta excavation (1887–9) 13, 140
Tell el-Dab'a frescos 32, 34–5
temples:
  Deir-el-Bahari 89, 93
  Khonsu 96
  Medinet Habu 95, 132
  Medinet Maadi 66
  mortuary 96, 132
  mythic reliefs 57
  offerings 132–3

Qasr el-Sagha *64*, 65–7
religious ritual 129, 131
Sebennytos 62
Seti I 117
Thebes 93
texts:
    Amarna period 148
    archaeological evidence and 79–81,
       88, 132–3
    Biblical links with 19–20
    ceremonial 75–6, 129
    funerary 118, 121, 126, 134–5, 143
    historical 56–7
    Osiris myths 116
    religious 132
    sebayt 135–6
Thales of Miletus 12
theatre 149, 156
Thebes 15, 56, 60, *61*, 69, 93
Thera (Santorini) 19, 34
thermal imaging 43
thermoluminescence dating 58, 65,
    68
Third Intermediate Period 56, 95, 122
Thutmose III 56, 57, 90, 91, 92
Tiye, Queen 152
Tomb 100, Hierakonpolis 82
tombs:
    artwork 34, 57, 82, 105, 108, *109*,
       119
    chambers 113–14
    chapels 108, 109, 110
    king-lists in 60, *61*
    royal 49–50, 96, 97
trade 37, 78, 90
Trans-Jordanian region 103–4
Trigger, Bruce 7–8, 26, 50, 98, 127
Tuna el-Gebel chalice *83*
Turin Canon 59–60, 62
Tutankhamun 36, 40–1, 42, 124, 158
Tuthmosis I 90
Tuthmosis III 87, 92
Two-dog Palette 4

U

Umm el-Qa'ab cemeteries, Abydos
    60, 63, 113

unification 4, 30, 48, 49, 54, 69, 74,
    103
Upper Egypt (southern region) 6, 10,
    49, 53, 78, 101, 135
Ursa Major 69

V

Valley of the Kings 105
Verner, Miroslav 144
viziers 5, 105, 135
von Daniken, Eric 142

W

Wadi Hammamat 45, 60
Wadi Maghara mines 90
Ward, William 63
water control 53
Weigall, Arthur 125, 145
Wepwawet, jackal-god 115
Wheatley, Dennis 123
White Crown of Upper Egypt 6,
    52
Wilbour, Charles 39
Wilkinson, Gardner 23
Wilkinson, Toby 102
Willems, Harco 69–70
Wilson, John 90, 119
Winlock, Herbert 69, 70
women:
    in Egyptian society 108
    Predynastic burials 121–2
    rulers 89–94, 110, 152, 154–7
    sexuality 111–12
Wortham, John 23
writing 32, 35, 39–40, 72–81, 88

X

x-rays 43

Y

Yadin, Yigael 103–4
Yaxchilan lintel 8
Young, Thomas 79